CW00953088

THIS IS THE
american
pit bull terrier
richard f. stratton

ISBN 0-87666-660-8

Distributed in the U.S.A. by T.F.H. Publications, Inc., 211 West Sylvania Avenue, P.O. Box 27, Neptune City, N.J. 07753; in England by T.F.H. (Gt. Britain) Ltd., 13 Nutley Lane, Reigate, Surrey; in Canada to the book store and library trade by Clarke, Irwin & Company, Clarwin House, 791 St. Clair Avenue West, Toronto 10, Ontario; in Canada to the pet trade by Rolf C. Hagen Ltd., 3225 Sartelon Street, Montreal 382, Quebec; in Southeast Asia by Y.W. Ong, 9 Lorong 36 Geylang, Singapore 14; in Australia and the south Pacific by Pet Imports Pty. Ltd., P.O. Box 149, Brookvale 2100, N.S.W., Australia. Published by T.F.H. Publications Inc. Ltd., The British Crown Colony of Hong Kong.

This book is dedicated to Bob and Doris Wallace

Contents

Chapter One

THE AMERICAN PIT BULL TERRIER

Civilize him as you please, make him whatever color you like, and Man will still worship the born fighter.

—John Tantor Foote

That is what Foote said in his story about a Pit Bull named Allegheny, and perhaps his words provide insight into the fascination elicited by the American Pit Bull Terrier. The breed is something of an enigma, for it has been known under many names, such as Pit Bulldog, Bulldog, Fighting Bulldog, American Pit Bulldog, Pit Bull, Pit Bull Terrier, Pit Terrier and, officially, as American .Pit Bull Terrier. Such a plethora of "aliases" makes for confusion among the public and has caused many writers to believe that more than one breed has been used in pit contests. Such is not the case. Others breeds—from Bull Terriers to Bullmastiffs and from Northern huskies and wolf hybrids to Akitas—have been tried and found wanting. It is not surprising that the Pit Bull reigns supreme once we learn that the animal has been bred for fighting and tested thereby for many centuries. Its bloodlines have been guarded and cherished throughout generations and from the dawn to the fall of civilizations all over the world. No one country or one age or one civilization can lay sole claim to this valiant breed. Should we wonder then that no other breed can stand in the way of a Pit Bull?

What *is* surprising to many people is that a breed that is such a threat to other dogs should have such an ideal disposition with people. The Pit Bull has to rank as one of the most affectionate of all dogs, and if raised as a house pet,

7

Riptide Rhoda, daughter of Wallace's Talking Boy, taught herself to sit up. She was a fine example of an alert and intelligent Pit Bull.

he will be a veritable lap dog, entertaining the family with tricks he has learned and with his generally clownish personality. One theory advanced to account for the breed's unusually stable and congenial-to-people disposition is that he is far too formidable a beast for it to be prudent to allow vicious individuals to survive (and thus to propagate). According to the theory, this selective process has tended to weed out the mean dogs and has left us with a dog with an almost ridiculously amiable disposition.

In spite of his gentle nature, the Pit Bull, because of his unusual abilities, is unexcelled as a guard dog. His appearance alone, with his robust build and his unafraid direct stare, is enough to deter the majority of would-be burglars. If more is desired, the breed is easily encouraged to protect property and people. The author must confess to a certain personal prejudice against attack-trained guard dogs for the simple reason that the record indicates that they bite women and children more often than they do burglars. However, it must be admitted that the Pit Bull, properly trained, is a guard dog *par excellence*—and he is less likely to bite the wrong people! In fact, the author knows of several cases where even intruders were subdued without being bitten!

A friend had always kept a Pit Bull as a guard for his business and a companion for his wife. (So satisfied was he with the breed through the years that he never even considered trying another.) Time after time, the dog proved his worth, yet he never hurt anyone. But somehow he conveyed the message that he could do untold damage if his hand were forced! A case in point, and a humorous incident to boot, was the time a policeman entered the back door of the owner's establishment uninvited and unannounced. (It was late at night, and the officer was checking out a crank call—and to top it off, he had the wrong building!) Unfortunately, Josh (the Pit Bull involved) discovered the intruder and was unimpressed by his credentials—

Rootberg's Josh, the dog that held the "uniformed burglar" captive for twenty minutes

even if he was in uniform! So he drove him back against the wall and kept him spread-eagled there for a good twenty minutes. Every time the officer went for his gun or tried to get away, Josh pushed his snout deep into his abdomen and gave a low and incredibly ominous growl. Now here was a case in which an intruder was subdued but completely unharmed, although, needless to say, he was quite happy to be rescued by Josh's owner!

Kelly's Susie, bred by Bob Wise

Picking at random other advantages of owning a Pit Bull, let us consider the vet bill. These dogs are downright "bullet proof"! Or, as an old friend used to put it: "You couldn't kill one with a hammer." What he meant, of course, was that individuals of this breed are hard to kill—either by disease or physical injury! A selective breeding process extending over hundreds of years has produced an exceptionally hardy and tough animal. The famous veterinarian Leon Whitney has made note of the fact that a derivative of this breed (the Bull Terrier) crossed with a distemper-prone breed (the Bloodhound) produced progeny that were highly immune to the disease. James Thurber, the famous writer and humorist, reminisced about his boyhood dog, a Pit Bull, and how the family became convinced that he was indestructible after he survived a series of accidents that would have been fatal to any other breed.

For those who become annoyed with barking dogs (and that surely must include ninety percent of the world population), the Pit Bull is pure pleasure! Unless encouraged to be "barky" by his owners or conditions, a Pit Bull is almost ghostly quiet. That doesn't mean that the breed is lacking in personality. To the contrary, Pit Bulls are born clowns and utilize all the doggy communication sounds; they just aren't out barking their fool heads off all the time!

Although not related to the spaniels or retrievers, the Pit Bull is an outstanding swimmer if given a chance to indulge in this activity. When I was a young boy, I used to take my old dog Spook on excursions to a lake along with a couple of friends. He loved to retrieve objects from the water, and he would even retrieve rocks that were thrown in by diving down beneath the surface to get them! (Sometimes we suspected he "cheated" by bringing back the wrong rock, but we could never prove it!) At times we amused ourselves by throwing larger items like large branches into the lake, and he always managed to bring them back. We were convinced that he would retrieve a telephone pole if we could only find a way to throw one in!

Even with all his attributes—and I have not mentioned them all, for we have other things to take up in this book—the Pit Bull is not a dog for everyone. For his legacy is a deadly expertise for killing other dogs. He may not even start fights, but he will most assuredly finish them! Therefore his owner must be willing to take the necessary precautions. Of course, most cities have leash laws now anyway, but a prospective owner of one of these dogs must be understanding about the Pit Bull's inborn urge to fight and be willing to be particularly careful to keep his dog separated from others. For the person who likes a well-put-together dog that can rough it with the best of them and yet has a gentle and affectionate nature, it will certainly be worth the effort.

Terry Hammond's Honcho

Chapter Two

THE CLINGING DEATH

You can't beat the pit dogs for courage.

—Stephen W. Meador

The somewhat dramatic title of this chapter was Jack London's name for the Pit Bull. Although a brilliant author, London was like most people in that he was a little confused about the breed and its nature. One of the purposes of this book is to provide a source of information for those people who would like to find out what the American Pit Bull Terrier is really like.

Just as a student of the Greyhound should learn something about dog-racing in order to more fully understand his breed and how it evolved, so should the person with a serious interest in the Pit Bull learn something about dog-fighting. If he finds the subject personally repugnant, he will "bite the bullet" and learn about it anyway, for if he really wants to understand the breed, he must learn the conditions of its formation.

To see the Pit Bull's fighting propensities in perspective, we should also take at least a quick look at territoriality in other animals. Nearly all animals fight, of course, but the fights differ in intensity to a remarkable degree. Ethologists have studied aggression in animals in order to understand the roots of the hostility in one of Earth's most vicious creatures—man himself! Surprisingly, most animals do not square off and fight as we think of them doing. Most of them rely on bluff (technically referred to as a "threatening display"). What is even more surprising is that some of the fearsome predators we think of as being so formidable will hardly fight at all! The Romans found

An old-time Colby dog

that out when they tried to stage fights between lions. Those high walls of the Coliseum were not there solely to keep the Christians from escaping; they also had to be higher than a fleeing lion could leap!

Most fights between predatory animals consist of a brief flurry that could hardly be described as anything more than a spat. They usually end when one of the participants "hightails" it! On the other hand, some of the more protracted and vicious intraspecific fights took place among such imposing animals as the common chicken! Another animal that fights fiercely is the dove—the symbol of peace! The dog, for whatever reasons, is one of the few predatory animals that performs moderately well; in any event, it was this species that eventually produced the greatest fighting animal of them all. Pound for pound, nothing else can hold a candle to a Pit Bull—not even a wolverine! Some poor misguided souls feel that this fantastic ability that has been bred into him makes the Pit Bull a freak. But is he really any more of a freak than other specialists, such as bird dogs, herding dogs, or trailing dogs?

Wallace's Hillbilly, son of Searcy Jeff

Creed's Iron Dusty, also known as Ross's Red Devil

**Going
Light
Rage**

Breeds with unusual abilities have been developed through selective breeding by intensifying and modifying to some extent that which was already present in their wild progenitors. For example, Border Collies herd sheep. Wild canids herd animals, too. . .in order to kill them! Bird dogs sniff out game with veritable telescopic noses. . .and wild canids do the same with not quite the same olfactory excellence. Guard dogs defend their masters' premises . . .and wild dogs defend their dens. Even lap dogs, with their playfulness and affection, have traits that have been refined from the normal sociability that wild canids display toward one another. And, of course, fighting is normal among all the wild canids, but it is not in the same class as that of the Pit Bull.

The ordinary canid, wild or domesticated, relies heavily on threat display in a fight:

1. The teeth are bared.
2. The hair along the back and around the neck stands out to produce an illusion of larger size.

3. There is a plethora of noise: growling and attendant sounds.
4. If it goes this far a further attempt is made to intimidate the adversary by rearing up and snapping, and finally even taking hold and possibly shaking.

If all these activities fail to stop his adversary, the normal canid, having shot the works, will usually make as strategic a withdrawal as possible—even if unharmed by his adversary!

Now let us take a look at the fighting characteristics the Pit Bull, the end product of centuries of breeding of the dogs that were the most successful fighters. One of the most striking differences is the almost complete loss of a threatening display:

1. A Pit Bull almost never bares his teeth.
2. If the hair on the back is raised at all, it is only during the first few seconds of a fight.

Hathaway's Hondo, 39 pounds of dynamite!

3. Remarkably, there is very little noise. There is almost no growling and sometimes none at all. (To the uninitiated, the quiet of the whole affair is downright spooky!)
4. A Pit Bull may rear up at the beginning of a fight, but he had better watch out! His opponent may out-maneuver him! Snapping (imaginatively called "slashing" by romantic writers of dog stories) does very little damage and is part of a threatening display. The Pit Bull takes hold, shakes and in general punishes with his hold; he releases it only to get a better one.

To sum up, then, the Pit Bull has almost entirely discarded the use of a threatening display. In turn, threatening displays do not impress him. He is not intimidated by large size, loud growls or flashing teeth.

As would be expected, the Pit Bull has a strong and agile body. He is incredibly tough, too. As someone once said, he is all piano wire and rawhide! He is hard to hurt and hard to kill. His size-strength-speed ratio is optimum. James Thurber tells a charming story of how he and his brothers used their boyhood Pit Bull to impress other boys in the neighborhood with the dog's prodigious strength and athletic ability. He would drag or pick up huge objects. He could catch on the fly any ball thrown as high as a boy could throw it. And at his owners' bidding he could leap extremely high walls and fences. All these feats will be familiar to anyone who has kept a Pit Bull as a pet.

Legendary strength, strong jaws and an ability to tolerate pain are the stock-in-trade of the Pit Bull. And they are important assets to a pit dog. However, there is something else pit dog men prize even more. To them the absolute top priority is *gameness*. Without gameness, ability is worth nothing. What is more, gameness—that absolute *dead* gameness—is hard to attain and hard to keep, which makes it all the more priceless!

Gameness is a term that is often misunderstood. It is, and has been, used by pit dog men for centuries to refer to the trait of never giving up, of never quitting regardless of punishment taken and regardless of how tired a combatant may be. It is important because it often intimidates the other dog. Many a pit dog has given up, and thereby lost a match, even though he was outfighting his opponent! A game dog that has good fighting ability will win a contest against another game dog that does not have equal ability. But many a game dog has defeated a bigger, stronger fighting dog that did not have sufficient gameness.

Pit dog men have always treasured gameness above all else for pragmatic reasons: the game dog wins over opponents that are not game. Strains that produce deeply game dogs are cherished and kept pure of others—even of the same breed. Occasional outcrosses to other strains are made in an attempt to obtain the bone-crushing pit artist. However, the deep gameness of such progeny is always suspect (even though they are purebred Pit Bulls of excellent strains) until it evidences itself in a fight.

Outcrosses to other breeds that I have heard of have always ended in disaster. Apparently gameness is polygenetic and thus easily lost in crosses to animals that are not game. (The progeny may be quarrelsome and fight longer than some other breeds, but that, of course, is not sufficient to win.) The reason the Great Dane or Bullmastiff does not win, as so many think he should, in a fight against a Pit Bull less than half his size is that he screams and runs when the Pit Bull clamps down on him. It is only natural that an occasional pit dog man would come up with a scheme to "make a little money off the boys" by challenging them with a hybrid, half Mastiff and Half Pit Bull, the idea being that the gameness afforded by the Pit Bull blood would carry the animal long enough to allow him to disable a smaller Pit Bull with his superior size and strength. Although the progeny often had prodigious size and strength, the gameness was never sufficient to win. So complete has been this failure that Pit Bull hybrids almost never appear in the pit now.

Knowing now how precious gameness is and how long it must have taken to attain that quality that the old time Bulldog possessed, can we really take seriously the old tale

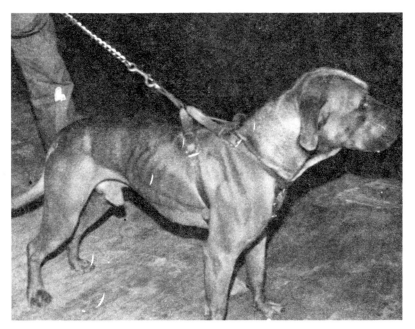

Broadway Jack's Champion Drummer

that the Pit Bull was produced by a cross of the Bulldog with a terrier? There is no reason to believe it! Early writings (the sole basis for the belief) are unreliable and self-contradictory. Paintings done 300 years ago show the "Bulldog" looking very agile and with a long muzzle. In fact, he looks like a Pit Bull! Pictures done about the same time also show Bulldogs with the pushed-in noses and screw tails. Apparently even in those days some strains were bred for an unusual appearance and others were bred for performance. The short noses, if we are to believe modern writers, were designed to allow the Bulldog to breathe better when he had hold of the bull. Don't believe it! The public has been hoodwinked by that idea for years. The Bulldog cannot breathe right even lying in his own bed, while the Pit Bull is able to breathe just fine regardless of what he has hold of—a boar, a bull or a dog!

Isn't it more logical to believe that our Pit Bull is a direct descendant of the old fighting Bulldog, with *no* crosses to dilute the all-important gameness? Maybe that is why he is often called "Bulldog" by pit dog men—even today.

Chapter Three

OLD WINE IN NEW WINESKINS

Anything but history, for history must be false.
—Sir Robert Walpole

Any long-established breed's history is suspect, because we simply have no way of knowing the actual facts of a breed's formation. In the case of our breed, I believe that the history of the (English) Bull Terrier was borrowed by early writers on the breed. (It was much easier to do that than be caught without a history!) In researching our breed's history, it is useful to keep these principles in mind: (1) Names tend to change. (2) Show dogs tend to change in appearance. (3) Dogs bred for performance are more likely to stay the same, although they have less lateral uniformity. (4) A brachycephalic dog, as pit dog men say, "has no mouth," so he would be useless for fighting or bull-baiting. (5) Artwork is our best "window to the past," because we are not always certain what writers of another age were talking about when they used breed names.

A series of articles by various authors tending to open up the question of the breed's history was published by *Bloodlines Journal.* They are reprinted here.

WHAT'S IN A NAME?*

It is common knowledge that even the devotees of the Staffordshire Terrier (the show counterpart of the APBT) were very unhappy with the name granted their breed by the American Kennel Club. They wanted the name— American (Pit) Bull Terrier—that the breed had been known by for over 100 years, but the (English) Bull Ter-

* Appeared in the September-October, 1974 issue of *Bloodlines Journal.*

rier was already firmly entrenched within the AKC, and English Bull Terrier owners lobbied successfully to prevent any other breed from using the name.

While the name American (Pit) Bull Terrier has been the accepted name by the majority of fanciers for at least a hundred years, it may come as a surprise to many to learn that it was not universally accepted when first adopted by the United Kennel Club. Many authorities felt that the breed should have a name of its own and that the term Bull Terrier should not be used at all. The problem was what name to use. The breed was (and still is) generally called "Bulldog" in casual conversations of most fanciers. The name American (Pit) Bull Terrier was (and is) in effect a formal name for the breed to be used primarily in print. Other nicknames occasionally used were "Pit Bull", "Pit Bulldog" and even "Pit Terrier".

This confusion of names is a direct result of the uncertain history of the breed. It is difficult to trace the history of nearly all breeds of dogs because of the paucity of references to specific breeds in early writings and because of the contradictions and ambiguities in the works on dogs produced by early writers. The history of the American (Pit) Bull Terrier is especially dark and uncertain because, even in ancient times, its activities and even its existence have been kept relatively secret. However, there are some references to fighting dogs even in writings that existed before the Christian era. When carvings, engravings or other representations of these animals are examined, it can readily be seen that they easily fall within the parameters of modern APBT stock. Also, paintings and woodcuts done of the original Bulldog show that it looked just like the modern American (Pit) Bull Terrier. If the Bulldog originally looked like our breed and was already agile like our breed, then the old story about the breed's origin being the result of a cross of the Bulldog and a terrier becomes an "unneeded hypothesis" and scientifically must be rejected on principle.

A student of any breed's history will find that he is in

Painting by various artists indicate that dogs similar to the American Pit Bull Terrier have been around for a long time. This painting of a 16th-century boar hunt was done by the Flemish artist Rubens.

for some monotonous times at the library poring over old writings that have only occasional references to dogs. He soon learns that old artwork is one of the most reliable sources of his research. He subsequently becomes a source of worry to his friends in art galleries or libraries when he looks right past nudes in paintings and concentrates on any dogs that might appear in the background. The thrill of discovery of pertinent data is made all the more sweet by the rarity of those occasions. It is the type of thing that can be downright addictive, and I find myself still engrossed in trying to ferret out facts about the breed's history. The following is the story of the APBT that seems to fit all the facts.

When mankind first used dogs for hunting, dogs and men were truly equal partners in the hunt. A group of men and dogs would work together in tracking and running the game down, and they even participated together in the kill. From these dogs came the coursing hounds, the scent hounds and the fighting dogs. In each of these groups there is a degree of specialization that has changed them considerably over the countless years of their existence.

The coursing hounds (best represented by the Greyhound) were bred for speed at the expense of their fighting and tracking ability. They were used mainly to run less formidable prey down (usually in a "sight chase") and to keep other prey slowed down until the human hunters could catch up. Representations of these types of dogs existed clear back in ancient Egyptian times.

The scent hounds (e.g. the Redbone, Walker, Plott, etc.) were developed to track and locate the game for the human hunters. It was not intended that they help kill the game, but they developed a marvelous tracking ability and a beautiful baying bark that communicated to their owners not only where they were tracking but (by changes in intensity and pitch of the bark) how close they were to the game.

The fighting dogs at first were probably kept on leash or carried to the spot and used once the prey had been located by the scent hounds. (They are still occasionally used in this way.) They had neither the swiftness of the coursing hounds nor the tracking ability of the scent hounds, but they were just as proficient in their area of specialization as the other dogs were in theirs.

It is interesting to note that the Bulldog was often referred to as a type of hound in early writings. He also was occasionally referred to as a Mastiff or Alaunt, so it is quite likely that those terms at one time all referred to basically the same fighting strain that varied in size and conformation somewhat throughout the world.

As early as 300 years ago, an aberration was developed from the Bulldog strains that was kept mainly as a curiosity, for it had a human-like appearance. This was the brachycephalic or "pushed-in nose" type. It was useless for fighting and bull baiting, for it did not have the long punishing jaws, but it was still called "Bulldog," because it

Going Light Jim

was simply a malformed specimen of the breed. Because of its comic appearance, it was more likely to be kept as a pet than its fighting brethren (who earned their living in the pit or hunt). The irony is that in the public mind the term Bulldog became associated with the malformed variety rather than the original breed.

About 1850 a man named Hinks (according to his son) produced the (English) Bull Terrier by crossing the pushed-in nose type of Bulldog with the Old English White Terrier (now extinct). Early drawings of some of the first individuals of this cross showed these dogs to have the retrorse nose of the malformed type of Bulldog. Selective breeding probably produced the longer muzzle that today's specimens have. So we find that the American (Pit) Bull Terrier is not as closely related to the Bull Terrier as was formerly supposed.

Because of the uncertain history of the breed, there has been much confusion created in the public mind about the APBT and its relationships to other breeds. The fact that breed names and nicknames have been used rather sloppily does not help things any. Consequently, the beginner in this breed has one whale of a time trying to get the names straight. With this fact in mind, I am providing the following glossary. Most of the information is accepted fact, but I have placed parentheses around my own conjectures—even though they are based on solid evidence!

GLOSSARY OF BREED NAMES AND NICKNAMES

(Note that accepted breed names are treated as proper nouns and are therefore capitalized. Breed nicknames are treated as generic terms and are therefore not capitalized. It is difficult to discourage the use of nicknames—especially when the formal name is as big a mouthful as our breed's—but my suggested treatment of nicknames will help us keep in mind that they are just that, merely nicknames.)

Champion Dirk, owned by Mike Myrick, is an excellent example of an American Staffordshire Terrier.

American (Pit) Bull Terrier. . . . The direct descendant of countless generations of game dogs. Although primarily famed as a fighter without equal, this breed has proved to be useful in predatory animal control and as a catch dog and guard dog—and it just so happens that he makes an excellent house dog!

American Staffordshire Terrier. . . . The show counterpart of the APBT. Except for some game strains that are dual-registered, these dogs could not be expected to be as game as the APBT or to have the same ability.

The brachycephalic-type Bulldog

Bull Terrier. . . . A show dog that was produced (around 1850) by a cross between the brachycephalic-type Bulldog and a terrier. Despite popular opinion to the contrary, this breed, because of insufficient agility and gameness, was never consistently used as a pit dog.

Bulldog. . . . The brachycephalic-type Bulldog now formally bears the name of his progenitor, the old original bulldog (now known as the American Pit Bull Terrier).

A Bull Terrier (white variety)

**Bull Terrier
(colored variety)**

Today the relationship to the APBT is extremely remote because the breeds have been bred separately for so long. In fact, about the only thing the breeds have in common is that they are both dogs!

bulldog. . . . Nickname for the American (Pit) Bull Terrier. (It is important to note once again that the APBT almost certainly was the original breed that was known as the "bulldog.")

pit bull. . . . Another nickname for the APBT, one that has been in use for at least 200 years (probably to distinguish it from the brachycephalic-type "bull.") To further confuse the issue, the Bull Terrier people sometimes use this term to refer to their breed, apparently in the mistaken belief that their dog is, or was, used in the pit.

Staffordshire Terrier. . . . former AKC name for the American Staffordshire Terrier.

Staffordshire Bull Terrier. . . . An English showdog that is descended from many of the same ancestors as the APBT. However, it has been bred along different lines from the American Staffordshire Terrier and has very little similarity to the American (Pit) Bull Terrier.

Yankee Terrier. . . . A name that was concocted when the AKC refused to register the American (Pit) Bull Terrier under its own name. For some reason, this name, too, was rejected.

THE AMERICAN (PIT) BULL TERRIER
A BRIEF HISTORY OF A GREAT BREED *

When the Roman legions conquered Britain, they civlilized the savages, built roads and temples and fortresses and towns, built aqueducts, laid a basis for the language we know today as English, and brought a sport, a sport that dated back to Minos in Crete, the sport of bullbaiting. This sport developed from the cult worship of a warrior god, Mithras, whose devotees signified his might as a young white bullock, the form he assumed to give courage to his followers in battle.

In those early days, there were many large ferocious dogs, usually wild, that were caught and used for the soldiers' sport. Through the years, the Romans were assimilated into the tribes they had conquered, or moved on to other campaigns, but their civilization and their sport lived on and continued to flourish among their descendants, the landholders and royalty.

Through those same years, the dogs became more typified, due to selective breeding for the Roman sport, and also due to the fact that only the strongest and most intelligent dogs survived the sport.

Let us now take a great leap through the centuries to the early 1700's—a time which finds a middle class firmly entrenched in English society, a class of merchants, gold-, silver-, and black-smiths, inn-keepers, tailors, bakers, etc. This class mimicked the fashion, customs and diversions of the upper classes, among them the sport of bull-baiting.

Let us also take a look into the canine world of that day. Now we can see types, almost true breeds: terriers, cattle dogs, shepherds, and a large dog, called Bull-Dog, (for obvious reasons) or mastiff which at that time meant "large dog." There was the terrible Blue Paul, from Scotland, and the just as terrible Alaunt, from Ireland, all come to test their mettle against the English bulls; they were bred with the great dogs of England, and their offspring baited the bulls. By 1800, the result of this breeding was a large long legged animal weighing 80 to 90 pounds, and, you must take into consideration, these dogs were not fed on a regular basis, to insure their ferocity against the bull.

The early 1800's were poor years for the men of the middle class; they could no longer afford the bulls for the ancient sport, and its popularity declined. In 1835, the sport was officially banned. A few followers of the sport defied the law and surreptitiously continued it for several years.

Law-abiding men, however, were busily developing a new sport, one not quite as costly, dog fighting. There were plenty of dogs left over from the bull-baiting days, huge dogs, ferocious

* Appeared in the November-December, 1974 issue of *Bloodlines Journal.*

dogs, but not quite fast or agile enough to make this new sport truly exciting.

Let us at this time look at a segment of English society we have overlooked, the lower class. These poor unfortunates had had from time to time serious vermin problems, namely rats, which they also found a remedy for: terriers. While our upper and middle classes were developing their great dogs for sport, the lower class was refining the terrier for survival.

Terriers, small, agile, lithe and sinewy, caught and ate their own food. Although small, they were deep-chested and powerful enough to dig the rats right out of the burrow. A terrier was a necessity to a poor man—any chicken-stealing fox or grain-thieving rat was fair prey to his terrier.

The terrier had his place in the poor man's diversion, a sport called "ratting"; rats were caught and placed in cages, a pit was dug, bets were placed, and the rats and terriers released in the pit. The dog catching and killing the most rats was declared the winner, and his owner went home jingling a pocket of coins.

Several types of terriers were developed, but only the ones pertinent to this history will be discussed. The English White Terrier, which became extinct in the early 1900's, resembled what is known today as the Manchester Terrier in size and conformity, but with a head that looks quite like the American (Pit) Bull Terrier of today. It was a very game dog, but perhaps not as game as the black-and-tan, which survives today in the Manchester Terrier, very little changed. There was the Fox Terrier also, a slightly larger, more burly type terrier, capable and adept at catching and killing the larger contenders for the farmers' food.

No one knows who first thought to breed the huge Bull-Dog with agile terriers, nor were accurate records kept, but apparently it was handled quite successfully by the coal miners and iron-workers of central England in the Staffordshire area and called the Bull-and-Terrier.

The Bull-and-Terrier quickly gained popularity among sporting men, as, owing to its more compact size, it was more easily handled, ate less and gave these fine sporting men the opportunity to participate. Rules were laid and usually abided by as a point of honor, but the very best facet of this newer breed was its terrier-like propensity toward mankind, which allowed the owner to be right in the thick of the sport, urging his dog with hands and voice, quite unlike the haphazard, strictly spectator bull-baiting. In the early days the sport took place in the old bull arenas, street corners, barns and sheds, but again the middle class was on the rise and took a fancy to the newer sport and the Bull-and-Terrier. Soon most every pub and inn had a small arena in a room to the side, or in the main room, depending upon the size of the establishment.

These arenas became known as pits, taken from the old lower class sport of "ratting," and, of course, fighting was soon called pitting, and winning dogs became known as "Pit Dogs." It became quite fashionable for the young dandies to be seen about town with a Bull-and-Terrier under their arm. Taking their dogs to a pub, it would be allowed to be on the bar for all to see and make wagers on, with the bar-keep or inn-keeper holding the money.

Meanwhile the old Bull-Dog was becoming quite rare due to being used up as a base stock for the newer more agile breed; only the few men dedicated to the old Roman sport managed to save the breed from extinction. These men were landholders and could well afford to buy a newly introduced dog from China that was causing quite a stir among the royalty of the day, the Chinese Pug. By breeding the Bull-Dogs and the Pugs, these men gradually developed the short-legged, kink-tailed, broad, squatty modern day breed we known as the Bulldog.

The Bull-and-Terriers from Staffordshire had gained a sizable reputation for their gameness and performance, and probably due to the close-knit mining community these dogs had a definite typiness; they became known as the Staffordshire Bull Terrier, but not until 1935 was this the official name, when the English Kennel Club designated it such and recognized it as pure-bred.

We are now going to go back in history once again, this time to the Western Hemisphere and the colonization of America and Canada. Wherever man goes he takes his dogs, and terriers were just as much in demand in the new world as in the old, as were the large, fierce Bull-Dog types needed to protect man from marauders. These men also needed diversion and looked to their dogs for sport. Through the years a type of Bull-and-Terrier developed here, a larger-boned, heavier dog than its English cousin.

Shortly before the Civil War, the English dogs were brought to America by merchants, sailors, and traders, and the sport of dog-fighting flourished in the port towns. The English and American Bull-and-Terrier types were cross-bred and refined through the concerted efforts of the sporting men.

Mr. C.B. Bennett, a renowned sportsman and fancier, as well as breeder, organized a stud book and registering office in 1898. He designated the breed name to be American (Pit) Bull Terrier. Mr. Bennett also established rules governing the pitting of dogs and set up the official breed standard as it stands today.

The United Kennel Club was established 77 years ago by Mr. Bennett for the sole registration of the American (Pit) Bull Terrier, and has grown to be the second largest dog registering office in the United States.

The American (Pit) Bull Terrier is considered to be the most powerful dog, pound for pound, ever developed, even though they

Don
Carter
and
Bullard's
Sarco

Sequan Willie, the *Schutzhund* dog

are also known for their devotion and steady temperament with humans. The versatility of the breed is perhaps its most outstanding feature. We all know of its reputation for prowess in the pit, so we will go on to other less known qualities.

The American (Pit) Bull Terrier has a natural inclination for hunting and has been trained to hunt everything from bird to wild boar. Its deeply ingrained fearlessness, stamina and high pain threshold allow it to take brutal punishment without a whimper; for this reason, it does not make a good bear or wild-cat hunter, as its tendency to lock its jaws on an opponent leads to the dog's destruction.

This breed is not known as an indiscriminate people-biter. It has the innate ability to distinguish between true aggression and play; therefore it is a good family companion that will offer protection when and if needed. It is unusually tolerant of small children and accepts their roughness as a matter of course, gauging the child's strength and playing in accordance.

Adaptability is a key word for this breed. The American (Pit) Bull Terrier is at home in a city apartment, a suburban split-level, a farm or a kennel. Owing to the extremely short coat, shedding is minimal; therefore the little grooming required is just keeping the teeth free of tartar, the ears free of mites and dirt, and the nails filed down to prevent tearing.

Centuries of depending not only on its strength but also on its wits for survival has produced a very high intellect in this breed. Due to this intelligence and willingness to please, the American (Pit) Bull Terrier is easily trained and very rarely forgets. The dog has a long attention span and a mind of his own, which often leads to him outsmarting his human owners.

In the early 1900's the American (Pit) Bull Terrier was one of the most popular breeds in America, as witness Tige, Buster Brown's companion in the comic strip, and the dog we still see today on R.C.A. products, purported to be Thomas A. Edison's faithful A.(P).B.T. During WWI the breed represented "Old Glory" on our allies poster, with the squatty English Bulldog as a representative of the "Union Jack" and the French Bulldog the "Tri Color" flag. No history of the breed is complete without mention of Pete, the ring-eyed canine, comic companion of the "Our Gang" kids. Pete has the distinction of being the first A.K.C.-registered Staffordshire Terrier.

Today we are again seeing a resurgence of popularity in this truly great breed, the American (Pit) Bull Terrier.

Cherie Kavanaugh
Pub. Dir. A.(P).B.T.C.S.C.
9084 63rd Street
Riverside, CA 92509

Curtis's Mike, a
pure Colby dog

Ackel's Nick

ADDITIONAL HISTORY OF THE AMERICAN [PIT] BULL TERRIERS * by L. Dillon

I was intrigued and somewhat bewildered by the literary efforts of Cherie Kavanaugh in the January-February edition of Bloodlines. *In that particular issue, C. Kavanaugh treats the reader to a dictionary definition of "sport." I would suggest that before she writes another "history" of the American (Pit) Bull Terrier — however brief — she researches the meaning of history. The students of history base their opinions on contemporary factual evidence, without which we have fiction. C. Kavanaugh in my opinion writes fiction.*

To illustrate my point: in her article "A Brief History Of A Great Breed," paragraph 1, she stated that the Romans brought bull-baiting as a sport to Britain. I challenge her to produce any firm contemporary evidence whatsoever of the historical validity of this statement. If she can not prove this first point then it makes nonsense of her second paragraph point "that the sport lived on," as well as her third paragraph point "that the dogs became more typified due to selective breeding for the Roman sport."

In paragraph 5, her statement "there was the terrible Blue Paul from Scotland" is wrong, understandably wrong but wrong nevertheless. The mining area of Seghill outside the city of Newcastle, England, was famous in the 19th century for its fighting Bulldogs. (They bore little resemblance to the present day monstrosity). The champion of these famous animals was a remarkable bitch owned by Jack Simms, which he called "Poll" (Poll or Polly was a very common female name at this time). Poll's fame was widespread in northern England, and Blue Poll became quite a common name. Thus Simms used to match his Blue Poll against Wardle's Poll, etc. A Scottish salesman named Cathey brought a number of these dogs back to Scotland, where they became fashionable, so much so that Morrison of Greenock, Scotland was exhibiting one in the late 1880's. When it is remembered how the Scottish dialect requires a decidedly rolled 'r,' it is (1) evident how the name Poll eventually became corrupted to Paul.

Paragraph 6 states that the early 1800's were poor years for the men of the middle class. . . they could not afford bull-baiting. The following paragraph suggests that dog fighting was a new sport developed as a consequence of the prohibition of bull-baiting in 1835. Both points are incorrect. This period was one of great and rising prosperity for the middle classes, and dog fighting was an old established sport.

The dog Pit in Duck Lane, Westminster, London, functioned on Monday and Wednesday evenings. Patrons who attended there on Wednesday, May 23rd, 1816 paid the large sum of two shillings admittance to see an eleven-year-old dog, the winner of thirty contests, and five to four favorite, fight a renowned two-year-old for a

* Appeared in the January-February, 1975 issue of *Bloodlines Journal.*

purse of fifty guineas — a princely sum in those days! (2) *The attached photocopy from "Life in London" published July 19th, 1821* (3) *will, without further comment from me, confirm my point.*

1 AN ITALIAN TURN UP.
Surprising Novelty in the Sporting Circle.

On Tuesday next, September 5, at Seven o'Clock in the Evening.
A special grand Combat will be decided at the
WESTMINSTER PIT.
FOR ONE HUNDRED GUINEAS,

Between that extraordinary and celebrated creature, the famed Italian Monkey,
JACCO MACCACCO,
of Hoxton, third cousin to the renowed Theodore Magocco, of unrivalled fame, and a Dog of 20 lbs. weight, the property of a Nobleman, well known in the circle.

N.B. The owner of the Monkey having purchased him at a great expense, on account of his wonderful talents, begs to notice to his friends of the Favor that another person has started a match, with a common Monkey, on the day preceding this match, with an intent to injure him and deceive the public.

After which, a Dog Fight, for Ten Pounds, between the Cambevell Black and Tanned Dog and the well-known Strafford Dog; and a match between two Bitches, the property of two Gentleman well known in the Fancy. To conclude with Bear Fighting.

Regular Nights, Mondays and Wednesdays

In paragraphs 8 and 9 it is suggested that the lower classes, in order to survive, developed the Terrier to kill devouring rats and hen-stealing foxes. In fact, the Statue of 1389 prohibited families with an income of less than forty shillings per year from owning a sporting dog. Apparently, prior to the Statute, the local lads had made serious inroads into the squires' game preserves with the assistance of sporting dogs (4).

I could continue but will conclude with one final point. In paragraph 13 C. Kavanaugh refers to the Dog Fighting Fraternity as "fine sportingmen." Yet on page 41 "To Those Who Fight Dogs," she seems to think that they are anything but fine!

1. The Illustrated Kennel News. December 15th, 1905.
2. Sporting Anecdotes. P. Egan. Published in London. January 1st, 1820.
3. Life in London. P. Egan. Published by Chatto & Windus, London. 1821.
4. Illustrated English Social History. G.M. Trevelyan. Published by Longmans, 1942.

Comments on the Breed's History *
by Richard F. Stratton

Several months back I presented in *Bloodlines* a slightly different view of the history of our breed from that which had been commonly accepted. (The truth of the matter is that no one had published any original research on the history of the American Pit Bull Terrier. Rather, most writers seemed to consider our breed a twin to the Bull Terrier, and simply borrowed the history of that breed and placed ours where they thought it would fit in that scheme of things.) Readers may recall that I pointed out that there was evidence that a fighting strain existed even in ancient times, and that it was known by many names depending on the time and geographic reference involved. Thus, Mastiff, Molossa, Bandog, Bulldog, Bullenbeiser, Baerenbeiser, Blue Paul (Poll), Red Smut, and a myriad of other terms may very well have all been applied to the same strain (and sometimes, perhaps, to variations of the strain). Now at what point we should declare this strain to be our breed is difficult to say, but paintings depict dogs (looking every bit like modern-day APBT's) engaged in combat with all manner of beasts, including other dogs, clear back in the 12th century!

Last month, Mrs. Cheryl Kavanaugh did an excellent job of explaining the traditional view of the breed's history. Now, following my articles as it does, her presentation may be confusing to the neophytes in the breed, but it provides me with an opportunity to point out some of the fallacies of the traditional (or show dog) theory of our breed's history. However, I want to emphasize that what follows should in no way be construed as a criticism of Mrs. Kavanaugh. What I am attacking is merely the historical view that was ably paraphrased in her article.

One of the main weaknesses of the traditional view is that it is based solely on writings done about the middle of the last century. There were few authors involved, and whatever they wrote must be considered testimonial evidence (generally considered the weakest form of evidence).

* Appeared in the March-April, 1975 issue of *Bloodlines Journal*.

Thus their writings provide a weak foundation indeed upon which to base any concept of our breed's origin.

Mrs. Kavanaugh states that when bull baiting was outlawed, fights between dogs then became popular and the old Bulldog was too large and lacked agility for this type of activity. First, there is ample evidence in paintings and woodcuts that fights between dogs as sport were no rarity long before bull baiting lost its following. The Bulldog was fought against every manner of beast—including lions! And there is no doubt he reigned supreme in dog-to-dog combat. As for his size, it varied—just as it does now (in the APBT). Naturally, the larger individuals would be favored for bull and bear baiting, but plenty of paintings show small individuals being used along with the larger ones. And there is no reason at all to believe that the breed lacked agility. After all, he had to be agile even for bull-baiting. I think it is safe to assume that he didn't best the bull by "outmuscling" him! It is probably true that in certain countries (such as Ireland and England) the smaller types began to be favored for pit fighting because they were easier to handle, easier to hide and cheaper to feed. However, all breeders had to do was select the smaller individual Bulldogs for their brood stock. There was no reason to outcross to another breed and thereby lose the gameness and ability that many centuries of selective breeding had achieved.

The various terriers that existed at the time of the alleged crossbreeding were referred to by Mrs. Kavenaugh as being game. In truth, there is really no reason to believe that. Would rats or other vermin test the gameness of a dog? Not hardly! (Stonehenge—probably the most respected of those 19th-century authors we have been talking about—lists the Bull Terrier under a section on "crossbreeds," and he seems to imply that the Bulldog was crossed with a terrier to increase the gameness of the terrier. Now, friends, it doesn't take much gameness for a dog to hang in there against a rat, so Stonehenge's comment is not very flattering to the gameness of his contemporary terriers!) As for the English White Terrier's resembling

Wise's
Massie

Kelly's BoJack,
Lightner-Mason
breeding

Wise's
Max

Sequan Maya in the type of kennel run that is ideal for an American Pit Bull Terrier

the Pit Bull, it is actually hard to say, but from the assortment of drawings and woodcuts I've seen, there is little resemblance. I assume Mrs. Kavanaugh is referring to the pictures in Rosenblum's little books on the Bull Terrier and the American Staffordshire Terrier, but who knows what that dog really is? No source is given.

Mrs. Kavenaugh also speculates that the old-time Bulldog was crossed with the Pug and thus begat his brachycephalic (pushed-in nose) form. To put that theory into perspective, let me say there are paintings depicting the brachycephalic Bulldog and writings describing it at least three centuries old. This is what muddies the waters for the student of the breed's history! There were *two* Bulldogs. One was kept as a pet or an oddity. The other was used for fighting, or hunting, or bull baiting, or for guarding the premises. (Of course, the "functional type" was probably kept as a pet, too, but not by the general public.) There probably *were* some crosses between these two types, but hopefully they were rare. In any case, the point is that the prachycephalic Bulldog has been around for a long time and was probably the result of selective breeding that began with random malformed specimens. The brachycephalic form was popular in several types of dogs (e.g. the King Charles Spaniel, Pug, Pekingese, etc.) because it presented an exotic and humorous appearance. However, in the Bulldog, it rendered him useless as a fighter, because such individuals had no biting power.

It is certainly true that the American Pit Bull Terrier is a good hunter and can sometimes trail fairly well—although, of course, not as well as a true scent hound. However, the breed is certainly not useless against wildcats. They seem to be capable of killing them almost as easily as a house cat. (Incidentally, I would like to interject here that hunting with an APBT may be more socially acceptable than pit fighting, but it is certainly more cruel. In a pit contest you have two animals bred to love what they do. Using Pit Bulls to hunt wild boar or wild cats—or whatever—involves inflicting a horrible death on an animal that most assuredly was not bred to like it!) Pit

Bulls are no match for a bear, of course, but the bear is not game and will often run from a Pit Bull upon experiencing the intensity of his attack. If you get a chance to see the movie *The Yearling* on television, watch it and you will observe a bear-hunt sequence in which a Pit Bull and a Black and Tan Coonhound corner a bear. The hound stays back out of harm's way snapping and baying. Although small, the Pit Bull closes with the bear and acquits himself admirably and manages to live through it. (The story of how the movie was made and where the dog came from is a story all by itself that I will save for another time.)

I think it is a mistake to say the method of fighting of the Pit Bull would lead to his destruction against a bear. Holding on in a fight is natural for all dogs. Romantic writers such as Jack London and Albert Payson Terhune have promulgated the mistaken belief that different breeds have different styles of fighting. Thus, the writers will speak of the "slashing" style of the wolf or the husky or the Collie as opposed to the holding-on style of the Bulldog breeds. What the writers have done is misinterpreted certain behaviors of dogs (or wolves) that they have observed. "Slashing" is a euphemism for snapping. And snapping is a component of a behavior that is technically known as "threat display." The reason a Pit Bull seems to hold on more than other dogs is because he has no threat or bluff in him and gets right down to business with very little or no threat display. "Holding on like a Bulldog" is a term that is not likely to be dropped from our language, but it is due to his gameness and not to a difference in fighting styles. I have seen huskies grab and hang on, and I have seen films of a wolf hanging on to the leg of a well-known ethologist to the extent that he had to be pried loose with what amounted to a breaking stick! (The wolf is a marvelous animal, and no dog can hold a candle to him in many respects. However, he cannot fight as well a Pit Bull any more than he can trail like a scent hound or herd animals like a Border Collie.)

Irish Jerry with Champion El Lobo

But back to the history of the breed. Some writers say the original Bulldog no longer exists. I say "Here is the original Bulldog (the APBT) come down to us from ancient times, retaining his original form and gameness, and he is truly a unique animal!" There may be critics of this view, and if so, so be it, for a little debate fans interest in the breed. Anyone who writes must expect his views to be criticized, and I most assuredly am not thin-skinned about having this happen. But I think the strength of my viewpoint in this particular instance is that I am simply stating the obvious. Thus, critics may find it more difficult than they think to chop down the lamppost!

Harry Clark with Kelly

Chapter Four

WHAT GIVES HIM THE EDGE?

The battle, sir, is not to the strong alone.

—Patrick Henry

As far as most dyed-in-the-wool devotees of the American Pit Bull Terrier are concerned, no breed of dog can hold a candle to the Pit Bull when it comes to fighting. That is a valid claim, but most fanciers become so enamored with the breed that other even more extravagant claims are also made. I have heard otherwise-sane people claim that the Pit Bull was unsurpassed in all areas, from birdhunting to sheepherding. And the claim is frequently made that the American Pit Bull Terrier is the ultimate all-purpose dog. Let me say here that the object of this book is to give the breed its just dues, but no attempt will be made to oversell it. To put the claim for the Pit Bull's being the all-purpose breed *par excellence* into perspective, let us consider the fact that nearly every breed of dog that was not bred for a particular purpose (e.g. herding, hunting, racing, etc.) has been touted as the great "all-purpose dog." In truth, these breeds are usually known to cyonologists as useless "meat burners"! Dr. Leon Whitney, in his book *The Truth About Dogs,* gives the story of the Weimaraner as one in which a breed was oversold as an all-purpose breed—which resulted in the breed's becoming a laughing stock among knowledgeable dog men. To be honest, the breeders did not really go to any great extremes. All they tried to do was to develop a breed that would trail game, point birds and make water retrieves. What they ended up with was a dog that was greatly outclassed by the specialists in all those areas. In fact, the activities of trailing and pointing worked against each other. It is easy to understand this when we learn that a *bona fide* bird dog signs his own death warrant if he *ever* puts his nose to the ground and gives any indication of trailing whatsoever! Now, as I understand it, modern Weimaraner breeders have gone a long way to rectify the mistakes of the early promoters. But I hate to see any dog campaigned as an "all-purpose" breed. There just isn't any such animal—not even the American Pit Bull Terrier!

It is true that individuals of our breed have distinguished themselves as retrievers or bird dogs or even as sheep dogs. But it must be understood that these individuals are *exceptions* and not the rule of what you can expect from the breed. I think one of the reasons some misguided fanciers have tried to promulgate the myth of the breed as an all-purpose dog is that its area of specialty happens to be fighting, and people have a tendency to play down that fact! But it is a fact that is of foremost importance in understanding the breed.

Countless centuries have been involved in developing the American Pit Bull Terrier into a fighting machine beyond comparison. And those persons who talk of other breeds surpassing him in this respect are merely displaying their own ignorance. Of course, not every single individual Pit Bull is proficient at what he was bred for; therefore, there are *some* true stories about Pit Bulls being bested in a fight. But generally speaking, such stories are fabrications of the same cloth as all the barroom stories that were once told by individuals of how they "whipped the Great John L. Sullivan!" Considering that some breeds outweigh the Pit Bull three times over, his dominance over them is a unique phenomenon, and it is all the more amazing when the breed's amiable disposition is taken into account. Far from being downplayed, the dog's fighting ability should be a source of open discussion and study.

Now as to what gives the breed that fantastic fighting edge, it is fairly obvious that the breed has an advantage in intuitive fighting ability. He has a built-in sense of leverage and a unique ability to work a hold to the best

Shorty Rowell with the pups "Sleep Easy" and "Smokey Dream"

possible advantage. His muscle quality and coordination are obviously superior to those of other breeds.

In terms of physical structure, we are all aware that the Pit Bulls of the past have varied, but they have generally

SHARKEY
A PIT BULL

1962

Sharkey (owned by Arther Lehman)

tended to have a somewhat stocky build, highly muscular but also fairly flexible. And, of course, one of the first things a newcomer notices about the breed is the generally large and rather ominous-looking head. The following is conjecture about the possible benefits of the physical makeup of the American Pit Bull Terrier.

Usually the stocky, muscular build is taken for granted as being the best because it is the strongest. But anyone who has dealt with these dogs for any length of time knows that the more slimly built dogs can be just as strong and may have an advantage in leverage. It is my own opinion that a slightly stocky build enables a dog to take punishment better, and it may also give him an advantage in speed (in terms of whirling, changing positions, etc.).

50

A large head seems to have obvious advantages. It makes larger jaws possible and provides a base for the musculature to service those jaws. One of the advantages of large jaws, besides the obvious one of providing more punishing power, is that of heat dissipation. A dog doesn't sweat like a human, but he throws off excess heat around his mouth. The more tissue exposed, the better.

The physical characteristics that have been mentioned are relative to other breeds and usually are not *extreme* differences. Somehow, extremes seem to work against a dog—which is something someone needs to tell the Staff people who, at the time of this writing, are breeding for exaggerated width and heads that are so large that their dogs nearly tip over forwards. The wide stance has been justified by the curious theory that it prevents another dog from throwing him. Actually coordination, fast footwork and a good sense of balance and leverage are what will really keep a dog from being thrown. But the truth of the

Riptide Cyclone, better known as "Honeybear"

Hammond's Ace, inbred Boudreaux dog off of "Bully Son"

matter is that it really is not that important whether or not a dog gets thrown. A good dog can protect himself from the bottom, and some dogs are seemingly happy to take the bottom in order to secure a favorite hold.

One thing more: I have heard Staff people down-grade the Pit Bull by complaining about the lack of conformity. The answer to that, of course, is that the breed is bred for performance, not conformation. However, the American Pit Bull Terrier has better longitudinal conformation than nearly all the show breeds. That means that the APBT looked the same over a hundred years ago as it does now, whereas nearly all the show breeds change with the changing whims of style, and their appearance a hundred years ago was considerably different. Just look at old pictures of Boxers, Mastiffs, or Collies! Another comment that I have heard from Staff people is that they had seen a pit champion (or his picture) and were disappointed that he did not have a large-enough head or wide-enough chest to suit them. The point these people miss is that the "scruffy little pit champion" they were berating very likely met and conquered wide-chested and big-headed dogs in order to gain his title!

In any case, as all knowledgeable pit dog men will tell you, the physical makeup of a fighting dog isn't that important anyway. The real difference that sets the Pit Bull apart from other breeds is inside his head. It is his unworldly love of battle that gives him his real edge. This love of battle has an intimidating effect on other dogs—especially if they are not Pit Bulls! There is just something about an opponent that keeps coming after you even after you've done everything you can do to him that is downright terrorizing! Some may think that this unholy love of battle is a psychotic condition, but it isn't really. (An indication that it isn't is that tranquilizers and other drugs do not qualitatively affect the fighting drive.) It is simply a matter of breeding. Others often feel that the Pit Bull is full of hate, but that isn't true either. Other dogs hold the same fascination for the Pit Bull as birds do for a Pointer or a raccoon for a Redbone Coonhound. The Pit Bull is *not*

Robert Stratton with "Socks"

a poor, unfortunate wretch, bred to be a freak. He is a happy dog, and life is full of excitement for him. How often have we heard the phrase "I felt so good that I felt like I could lick the world!" Well, the American Pit Bull Terrier feels like that all the time!

So strong is this love for battle that a well-bred individual of this breed will never cease fighting, not even when taking a beating, not even when tired and thirsty and hot. This is the trait that is called gameness by pit dog men, and it makes the breed indomitable! It is manifested when you have to save a small individual of the breed from a larger one that had him down throttling the life out of him. If he is a typical Pit Bull, he will cry pitifully to·get back to the other dog and will act as though he is completely convinced that *he* was the one in command!

And, as a matter of fact, a good game dog somehow has a way of winning while seemingly taking a beating. There is just something about a game dog that makes him hard to hurt, hard to kill and hard to whip. Part of it, no doubt, is due to the fact that he never gives the other dog a rest; since he never gives up, he is keeping his opponent so busy the whole time that he isn't able to inflict punishment as he normally could.

Hard bite and good wrestling ability are important, but

Hammond's Willie

**Willie
the
Protector**

gameness is. . .everything! The name of the breed is game. It is the single characteristic that most decidedly sets the breed apart from all the others.

As mentioned earlier in the book, gameness is a term that is often misunderstood. Although it is not synonymous with aggressiveness, there is an aspect of gameness that involves considerable self-confidence on the part of the dog. It is true that many Pit Bulls are "fight crazy" and will grab anything that moves (except people). However, the same dog that will grab a cat will also jump right at the middle of a lion or a bear. Foolish, perhaps, but it is amazing what these dogs are able to pull off because of their tremendous self-confidence and enthusiasm. There was a story told in one of the news magazines right after the Seven Day War in Israel that reminded me of the American Pit Bull Terrier. It was about two Israeli soldiers who went bounty hunting for Arabs after a mopping-up episode. Well, it seems that our two freelance soldiers had a luckless day, not spotting a single Arab, so they bedded down for the night in a small valley. At sunrise the next day, one of the sleepy-eyed pair crept out from the tent. Glancing up at the horizon in all directions, he discovered that their position was surrounded by Arabs poised for the attack. They were a tough-looking bunch with knives in their teeth, long curved swords in their belts, and a variety of firearms. They radiated malevolence, and they boasted a numerically impressive band. The Israeli rushed inside the tent to awaken his companion. "Abe," he cried, shaking him, "Wake up! We're rich!"

Well, the typical Pit Bull has an attitude like that. And who is to deny that he is rich! He apparently never feels defeated. That is probably part of the secret of his deep gameness. Another part of it is that he seems to enjoy fighting contact, even when he is getting the worst of it. The well-known Pit Bull fancier J. L. Colby once told of a

Mongol King and "friends"

Cable's Fang

Kelly's Dee

dog dying of old age that was taken off his chain and laid out in the yard to allow him to breathe his last in as much comfort and dignity as was possible. Finding himself loose, the old dog dragged himself over to the nearest dog, and they had one whale of a time getting the dogs separated!

But a dog doesn't have to be fight-crazy to be game. And certainly not all fight-crazy dogs are game. "Fight-crazy cur" is a common expression that refers to the countless Pit Bulls that have only limited gameness. That is, they will be crazy to fight, then quit in as little time as ten minutes. Then, after a brief rest, they will be just as crazy to fight again! The point is that aggressiveness towards other dogs cannot in any way be utilized as a barometer to determine a dog's gameness. Many deep-game dogs won't even bother with little dogs or even big dogs that don't challenge them. For that reason, Staff people or even Pit Bull fanciers that pronounce their dogs game strictly on the basis of a dog's aggressiveness are simply whistling in the wind!

Chapter Five

SHORT AND TALL TALES OF THE PIT BULL

You ain't heard nothin' yet, Folks!

—Al Jolson

Actually, all the stories in this chapter are true with the exception of one which I'll let you discover for yourselves. For those folks who are new to Bulldogs, these stories should provide glimpses into the nature of the breed. As for those who are not new to the breed, they are so busy telling stories about the dogs that I can't get a word in edgewise. Now it's my turn!

As a youngster in a small town in Colorado, I used to listen to stories about Pit Bulldogs that were told by two "pillars of the community" who at one time had indulged in a little sport with the dogs. Although neither of these two successful businessmen had any Bulldogs at the time I knew them, they obviously had never lost their love for the dogs and seemed to be happiest when they were telling stories about them.

A central figure in many of their stories was Jocko, a 28-pound brindle dog with white markings. Although Jocko was small in size (typical of the Irish dogs brought over to this country in the last century), he was 28 pounds of dynamite! Although he loved people and was friendly with everybody, he had a roguish personality and a penchant for mischief that was forever getting him and his owner into trouble. For one thing, Jocko stalked other dogs the way most dogs stalk cats. He wasn't allowed to run free, of course, but he had an intelligence and an absolute lack of morality that compensated for that fact. For example, when kept on a cable, he would stay at one end of the cable, pretending he was secured at that end. As soon as a dog was lulled into range, Jocko charged like a shot! He would also lie on his back, pretending to be asleep, and wait for a dog or cat to come within reach of his chain. Jocko, ahead of his time, had set up his own animal control center!

Jocko had several owners because, with his roguish personality and penchant for causing trouble, nobody could stand him for too long at one stretch! Everybody admired him, though, and some people, gluttons for punishment, even owned him more than once.

In a story I remember as being practically classic in that it described a typical Jocko antic and at the same time revealed his total love of fun and complete lack of conscience, Jocko was the proud possession of a professional boxer. This fellow was extremely fond of Jocko and obviously felt a certain community of interest with the dog. The two enjoyed each other's company immensely, and Jocko even got to do roadwork with his owner. Our story concerns how Jocko managed to terminate this happy arrangement.

It seems that Howard (our boxer) had taken Jocko in his buckboard wagon (this was around the turn of the century) to the outskirts of town (where there were no dogs) and the two had done their roadwork. Returning to town in the buckboard, Howard passed his friend Sam, rounding the corner on foot in the opposite direction. Howard, a friendly sort, waved a hearty greeting. And this was the moment Jocko had been waiting for! Apparently, he had been fascinated all along by the reins that moved and snapped so tantalizingly! True to his nature, Jocko concealed his interest in the reins until an opportune moment. Now, with Howard's attention diverted to Sam, Jocko seized the reins in his teeth and commenced a series of shakings that made those reins snap as they had never snapped before! The horse's head received the brunt of the punishment that Jocko was administering, and, of course, the animal bolted, completely out of control!

All that Sam knew was that he was waving to his friend

Howard when, all at once, the wagon seemed to be enveloped in a whirlwind, then the vehicle disappeared in a dash around the corner. Concerned, Sam ran after it. Rounding the bend, Sam blinked incredulously at the sight that was now before him. The wagon was on its side in a heap, one of its wooden wheels sticking up above it all and still spinning. Howard was in a smaller heap a few yards away from the wreckage. Although slightly dazed, Howard was glowering in the direction of that still-turning wooden wheel. For, there, perky as ever and not a scratch on him, was Jocko biting at the spokes of the wheel as it turned!

Bumatay's Sumatha, owned by Norman Gonsalves, is an oversize replica of the old dog Jocko (of whom there are no existing pictures).

THE BULLDOG AND THE STATUE

The great breeder Bob Wallace used to tell a story about his dog Spike, the Pit Bull he had when he and Mrs. Wallace were married. Spike was Delaney ("Danger Boy") and Dunable breeding, and he forever retained a special spot in Bob's heart.

This particular story begins with Bob sitting in the office of a Pit Bull enthusiast and veterinarian, Dr. G. Mayo, and Bob doing a little bragging about his dog. It seems

Wallace's Spike, the Bulldog that tangled with a statue!

that Spike had shown signs of being a pacifist in his younger days, and when street curs would challenge him, he just avoided them or retreated behind Bob. But now, his dog had definitely come of age, and Bob was saying that Spike would tackle a locomotive if encouraged to do it. Dr. Mayo chuckled and pointed to something he thought that Spike would be afraid of. It was a life-size plaster of paris (English) Bulldog. Dr. Mayo had kept it in the waiting room of his office. The veterinarian had often been amazed by the cringing reaction to the statue of large and powerful dogs that visited his office. There was something about the steadfastness, the smell, the immobility or whatever that seemed to elicit a frightened reaction in all dogs. The men decided to put the question to a test.

Bob brought Spike into the office, and Dr. Mayo took the statue into one of the examining rooms. At a word from Bob, Dr. Mayo opened the door into the hallway of the waiting room and slid the statue out, and Bob released his dog. Spike was upon the statue like a shot; he took hold and began shaking it. All parts of the room—including the ceiling!—were sprayed with fragments of the disintegrating statue, as Spike literally pulverized his "opponent"! As Bob, Dr. Mayo and his kennelman surveyed the wreckage, we can only imagine the glow in their eyes that men reserve for the born fighter.

JOCKO AND THE BOBCAT

Although I am convinced that pit dog men are wrongly accused of cruelty to animals by those who are not familiar with the American Pit Bull Terrier breed, I am very much against the fighting of a Pit Bull against a wild animal because, in such a situation, you have an unwilling participant or, in most cases, an animal that is simply fighting for its life.

Just as a point of interest, however, the little dog Jocko (previously referred to) was at one time pitted against a bobcat that actually outweighed him. Jocko tipped the scales at 28 pounds. The bobcat was kept by a saloonkeeper in Colorado. I'm not clear how they managed to weigh the bobcat, but he was reputed to weigh 35 pounds. Surprisingly, most of the men seemed to feel the bobcat might take Jocko, but then, none of the men were seasoned pit dog men. In any case, Jocko killed the bobcat very quickly by crushing its skull.

Pit Bulldogs are often used for hunting, and the general consensus seems to be that no animal anywhere near their size seems to have a chance against them. It might be of interest to know that writings done hundreds of years ago seem to indicate that it took three Bulldogs to kill a lion and four to kill a bear. That is still giving away a tremendous amount of weight, since three dogs would only weigh around a hundred and fifty pounds. I have a certain amount of skepticism about such statements, since it would be hard for the dogs to hold the lion there to kill once the big cat had decided to "break for it." I could certainly live with the statement that three Bulldogs could normally *defeat* a lion, although such things are only of casual interest to me.

CURLY AND THE SNAKE

Curly was a 47-pound pure Old Family Red Nose dog that functioned as a house pet for Bob Wallace and his wife, Doris, for over ten years. It was my pleasure to see this dog in his home in 1957, and he was truly an admirable animal, smart as a whip and one of the most beautiful Pit Bulls I have ever seen. Bob once made out a thumbnail sketch on Curly and a number of other dogs, and this is what the one on Curly said:

"Kennel Name: Curly

Registered Name: Wallace's Red Brave

Kennel Weight: 55 lbs.

Pit Weight: 47 lbs.

Color: Red, red nose, red eyes, red toe nails

Comments: An old-headed dog from the time he was a pup. Very serious minded and seemed to understand everything that was said to him. Was never house-broken—yet never soiled the floor in his life. In going through any door, even from one room to another, he would stop and wait for permission to go through. He went with me every place I went, riding in the back of my station wagon with his head on my shoulder. He always walked close by the side of my leg like a Seeing Eye dog and obeyed every command instantly. He helped with all the chores, and at night he would get up two or three times and check the house, then come back and sleep in his bed beside mine. He got into several accidental fights with my other dogs as he was growing up, but these were always stopped, as he was always *murdering* his opponent. When he became mature and I had to know about the depth of his gameness, I tried him against two fighting dogs (both heavier than he), Rusty (little brother to Brindle Jeff) and Chief (a litter brother to Curly's sire). I sent him 1 hour and 18 minutes and nearly killed him. He crawled to complete his scratch at the end of that time, and I declared him game and one of the greatest dogs I ever produced. He could do it all, as he

Wallace's Red Brave, better known as "Curly"

was a gifted wrestler and hard biter, and he was game. But he was my baby, and I loved him like a child, and for that reason I never matched him. I was afraid I might send him too far and lose him. To have done so would nearly have killed me."

In a later letter, Bob told of how on a trip to Fort Smith he stopped the car to let Curly out to "do his duty." "Curly started jumping stiff-legged through the tall grass like he does when he is after a grasshopper. When he does that, I tell him to 'get it for Daddy', and he does! He has brought me toads and grasshoppers just like a bird dog. Without thinking, I told him to get whatever it was he was after— and he did! He came out of that grass with a four-foot water moccasin that he was holding about a foot and a half from the end of the tail, leaving plenty of room for the snake to twist and bite him. I was terrified speechless, but the old boy seemed to realize that the snake could be a danger, and he shook it so hard that he fell down on his elbows. But he never stopped shaking, and after a few minutes the snake was quite dead, his head smashed just as flat as if it had been done with a shovel. Mrs. Wallace nearly fainted when I had Curly carry the snake up to the car to show her!"

MIKE AND THE AKITA

In telling this story, I should mention that, generally speaking, it is not good form among most pit dog men to tell stories about a Bulldog whipping other breeds of dogs. First, it is considered the mark of a novice, and, in addition, as the highly respected breeder Howard Heinzl once observed, it is like a boxer bragging about beating up a Ping-Pong player. Or a black belt practitioner of the martial arts ticking off his conquests of baseball and basketball players. Finally, many pit dog men believe that it is not good for a Bulldog, especially an unschooled pit dog, to fight a cur (i.e. any breed other than a Pit Bull), as he may develop bad habits. Still, the occasional mixed matches are of interest—expecially in view of the fact that there are *always* some ignoramuses who think that they have found a breed that can beat the Bulldog at his own game.

It might be of interest at this time to put into perspective a Bulldog's fighting ability. Over thirty years ago, Louis Colby wrote me that the American Pit Bull Terrier could whip any breed regardless of weight. While I've never found reason to doubt that statement, we must remember that not every single Pit Bull is gifted with gameness or ability, and some will not fight at all. Naturally, there are some rare individuals that could be whipped by the house cat or a Poodle. Another consideration is the variability of size in the breed. Some strains run extremely small, with the pit weight of many individuals being as low as 28 pounds. While it would be unrealistic to expect such little fellows to take on all comers regardless of size, many of them are pretty tough customers, and one of the most vivid memories is of an individual this size roundly castigating a German Shepherd that had attacked him. However, it would be unrealistic to expect these dogs to consistently conquer dogs that are big enough to kill them before gameness can become a factor. After all, as someone once said about expecting too much of these dogs, "After all, they are only *human!*"

Still it is a very exceptional thing for a Bulldog to be whipped by another breed. The very few cases I have been able to authenicate involved, almost without exception, a very large dog against a much smaller Bulldog that was not game. In my opinion, the breeds with the most chance to have an occasional success against a Bulldog are the Tosa (a very large Japanese fighting dog, but one that has been stopped by the Bulldog in every encounter that I know anything about) and the Akita, another Japanese breed.

For nearly twenty years now, the Akita has been touted by some people as a dog that could whip the old Pit Bull. It was claimed that the Akita was used for fighting in Japan, and since it was a breed that outweighed the Pit Bull two or three times over, it seemed logical to think that the breed would have a pretty good chance against him. Even pit dog men conceded the possibility. The assumption was that the breed, being bred for fighting, would have at least a minimum of gameness. In recent years, there have been a number of encounters between· the two breeds. The following is typical.

A group of Akita owners had reached the point of wanting to test their thesis that the Akita could indeed humble the mighty Pit Bull. These owners approached the only Bulldog owner they knew, and he happened to be a man with only one dog. His dog was young and had never even been rolled before, but the Pit Bull owner was willing to oblige the Akita people, and they arranged to meet at a secluded spot in the country.

The Akita was brought down off the truck, and his appearance was so impressive and lion-like that our Bulldog man couldn't be blamed if he had second thoughts at this stage of the game. After all, this particular Akita had a bad reputation and was reliably reported to have killed a Doberman Pinscher. However, the Pit Bull fancier remained confident and brought his dog, Mike, out of the car. The Akita was released and approached stiff-leggedly and growling menacingly. At this moment, Mike's owner released him.

So swift was Mike's charge that he actually went right through the Akita, knocking him sprawling and overrunning him. Mike scrambled back around and got the Akita by the rear foot and proceeded to shake out the hold. As you will recall, Mike was a young dog that had never been schooled, so he was all exuberance and hustle, but he was a little short on "savvy." Consequently, he did a few crazy things like going into the side of the Akita's neck where there was nothing but hair. After wasting some time there, however, he got in on the brute's shoulder, and it was at this point that the Akita tore away and ran back to the truck. Mike's owner alertly grabbed him up and put him back on his leash.

Needless to say, the Akita owners were somewhat abashed at the poor performance of their pride and joy against a dog half his size. They had been imbued with the idea that the Akita reigned supreme in fighting ability, and they themselves had helped promote the image of the Akita as the conqueror of the Pit Bull. Such ideas that have long been held don't die easily, and as the group studied their dog cringing in the back of the truck, one of them had an idea. "Maybe," he said, "The dog has established priorities. Maybe he is simply protecting the truck. Bring that Pit Bull over here."

Mike's owner obligingly brought him over, but kept him on his leash. As soon as they got within five feet of the truck, the Akita very ignominiously abandoned it and ran into the hills!

THE BIG YELLOW DOG

Among all the confidence games that are run against the general public, there is at least one that utilizes an American Pit Bull Terrier. Although, I suppose, a little imagination could produce variations of the basic mode of operation, the swindle basically involves a man and a dog working together. It helps if the man is an older man and can pose as an alcoholic. The point is that the man needs to give the impression of being an easy mark, somewhat addled and given to boastful overconfidence. Simply put, our con man (sometimes called a "tramp dog fighter" by pit dog men) tours the rural areas of the country, occasionally stopping in at a small town; while pretending to be drunk and overly enthusiastic about his little dog, he cons the inhabitants of the town saloon into putting a little money on the town tough dog (German Shepherd or whatever) in a fight against his dog.

Mongol King fought and defeated all comers, including 137-pound Tosas from Japan and Chindo dogs from Korea, but never had the chance to prove his ability against another Pit Bull.

Jone's Tuffy

Riptide Jerry

**Wise's Sister Sue,
granddaughter of
Red Devil**

Now it might be of interest to fanciers that the last thing one of these tramp dog fighters wants is a tough-looking dog. For that reason, his dog is very unlikely to have an ear trim, and he probably will be some color other than brindle. Also, smaller dogs are preferred, and this is definitely a case where the more innocuous and scruffy-looking the Pit Bull is, the better!

As we pick up our story, Old Irish Mike (our tramp dog fighter) has just arrived in a small rural town in the mid-western part of the country. Old Mike made enough money on his last swindle to last him nearly a month. As luck would have it, Mike had happened upon an unusually gullible group at his last town. Their dog had been an unusually large one, probably half German Shepherd and half Airedale was Mike's best guess. Because of the size of their

Blanchard's Kwesi, 50 pounds

animal, the townspeople had little reason to doubt that he would deal with this newcomer in the same way that he had dispatched other dogs of similar size. Nor, when the dogs were released, did the townspeople have reason to doubt the sagacity of their wagers, for their brute had the little dog down, and it looked like he would soon be a goner. Gleefully, they doubled their bets, and they were only a little surprised that the little dog's drunken owner covered all their bets. They *were* considerably surprised, however, when ten minutes later, the little dog maneuvered his way to the top and, seizing their dog by the nose, threw him hard and began shaking out his hold. Shortly thereafter, their dog began crying loudly, then finally tore away and proved that, at least, he could outrun the little dog. Sadder but little wiser, the townfolk paid off Old Mike and only wondered privately how on earth a wandering drunk had ever come across such a gifted little fighter.

Now, as Mike wandered casually into his new town, hoping for another bonanza, he was somewhat disappointed not to spot any large bully dogs roaming the streets. A "local hero" was an essential part of his scheme. As a matter of fact, Mike noted, there weren't *any* dogs on the streets. On entering the saloon, though, Mike breathed a sigh of relief, for there in the middle of the barroom floor lay the biggest old yellow dog that Mike had ever seen. Certainly, the folks in this town would bet a pretty penny on that bruiser!

The townspeople turned out to be even easier marks than Mike had expected, for they soon had a match arranged with heavy money riding. Old Mike hauled his little buckskin dog out into the street under his arm. The townspeople followed after him with their big yellow dog. Big was the word, Mike noted, because outside, with the dog on his feet, he could see just how big that yellow dog was! Mike had a momentary concern for his little dog, but then he shrugged. Throughout his eight years of experience at running this racket, Old Mike had developed a pragmatic confidence that a Pit Bull could overcome any dog regardless of size. But when the dogs were released, the big yellow dog crushed the life out of the Pit Bull.

Petronelli's Fox, out of Carver's Pistol and Carver's Miss Spike

In a state of shock, Old Mike paid off his bets. When he finally regained his power of speech, the old Irishman asked "Say, what kind of dog is that?"

"We don't really know," replied the bartender. "My uncle in Africa sent him to me as a pup a few years ago. He's been a good dog. All he does is sleep all day. He sure does eat a lot, though, and he grows so much hair around his neck that we have to shave it off every summer!"

(So, okay, you win. This *is* the story that isn't true! It is an old pit dog joke that has been around for a long old time.)

Hammond's Nina, owned by Roy Chambers

DUSTY

As I recall, in the late 1940's the Bulldog situation in Denver, Colorado was about like this. Nobody worried too much about perpetuating a strain, for this was Lightner country and nearly everyone had Lightner dogs. Consequently, the number of dogs kept by each individual dog man was not large. There was a plasterer with two dogs, a saddle maker with four, a bricklayer with five, and a rancher with three or four. I believe in five years' time there was a grand total of one pit contest for money. These guys had fun with their dogs, but they were serious about them and took good care of them. They were about as guilty of cruelty to animals as a Greyhound man who takes his dogs out for a run occasionally.

In any case, one of these guys, Pete the plasterer, had a Lightner dog named Dusty. He was Pete's pride and his house pet. Dusty was an ear and leg fighter, as I recall, and was a better-than-average pit dog. Like so many Bulldogs, though, Dusty was gentle with people, and he loved everybody. He was a small dog with a gentle appearance that belied his fighting ability.

It so happened that Pete once sold a litter of pups sired by Dusty. One of the pups was sold to a fellow workman, and as the pup was growing up, the other guys began to kid this fellow about his big, bad "fighting dog," because like Dusty, this pup looked like anything but a fighter! The kidding got pretty heavy, and everybody started giving Pete the business about having sold the guy a bill of goods. While all of this was just good-natured fun, Pete decided to bring Dusty to work so the boys could see what a full-grown pit dog looked like.

Well, as could be predicted, the members of the crew were no more impressed by Dusty, with his soft silky ears and friendly mild ways, than they had been by his pup. (It is somehow reminiscent of how people were unimpressed by Frank Gotch, the heavyweight wrestling champion around the turn of the century when professional wrestling was still a legitimate sport. He wasn't big, and, as a matter of fact, he just looked like a good old farm boy. But he was a terror in the ring!) Pete left Dusty tied to a trailer out back, and periodically a workman would come in and, with mock concern, tell Pete that he better get out there because a Cocker Spaniel had his dog cornered. After several such reports, a man came rushing in who was not kidding. "Pete," he said, "You better get out there. Dusty's killing a dog!"

Everybody dropped their tools and rushed out. As it turned out, some mongrel dog had run afoul of Dusty and was paying the price. Dusty had him up in the air, shaking the life out of him. Pete immediately got Dusty loose with a breaking stick, and the mongrel scampered home little the worse for wear. But the workmen were duly impressed. In fact, some of the same fellows who were petting Dusty and kidding Pete about his dog being such a pansy were now afraid to even get near that same dog. Thus, in the twinkling of an eye, Dusty went from 39-pound weakling to 39-pound vicious killer! Of such illogic is public image made!

The last story in this chapter was originally written for *Bloodlines* by Cheryl Poston. She is a kinsman of mine in the sense that she, too, was raised by an American Pit Bull Terrier.

VINO, MY VICTOR *

At the risk of ridicule, I would like to share my unbelievable experiences with the readers of *Bloodlines*. These experiences are about a fantastic American (Pit) Bull Terrier.

"When I was only three years old, I kept "borrowing" our neighbor's (retired Air Force man) puppy. I will bet I "borrowed" that puppy ten times! Mother spanked me each time. The man finally gave her to me. We named our A.P.B.T. puppy VINO.

A year later, Vino pulled me out of Onion Creek (near San Antonio) by the seat of my pants. Well, we both had a

Sleep Easy and Smokey Dream

little growing up to do. When I was nine years old, living in East Texas, I was on the porch petting a German Shepherd, when suddenly he turned vicious—his eyes went blood red and he was foaming at the mouth. He was rabid! I jumped, to run, and fell screaming for Vino. By that time the German Shepherd had taken a pretty good bite out of my back. I remember lying there and all I could see was the white streak on Vino's neck as she climbed a 10-foot

Bumatay's Brutus, 90 pounds

Wallace's Baldy and Wallace's Brutus (litter brother to King Cotton)

"Baldy" (white)
U.K.C. 289-872
Litter Brother to
Hadleys Tinker
(Booger Red)
Apr. 28, 1946.
Galveston, Texas

"Brutus" (Brin.
Wt. 35 lbs.
Litter Brother t
King Cotton
Galveston, Texa

fence, which was used to contain Brahma Bulls, to get to me. Vino took the dog's whole back off. Then my uncle finished off the German Shepherd with a bullet. It is commonly known that a dog will not attack a rabid dog, but Vino did! Vino and I both took the rabies injections.

A few years later, while I was riding my bicycle, two Great Danes came at me, biting at the tires and my feet. Vino promptly removed the left front shoulder from one and I kept on peddling. I had grown accustomed to my protection by then. She was not really vicious unless I was endangered. She loved all children and even tried to nurse orphan pups.

Vino would sometimes come to school to find me, and when I changed classes she would change windows to stare into. Under the teacher's orders, I would have to tell her to go home; she would start going, but she'd pause every few feet to give me a dirty look. She had human expressions. I swear she could smile. I came home many times to find Vino gone. She would go to my aunt's house when she was mad at my grandmother. So I would call on the phone and they would put the receiver to Vino's ear and I would tell her to come home. She would be there in ten minutes. My aunt said she would tear at the door until it was opened. Also, if we talked of where we were going, in front of her, we often got there to find Vino waiting for us "smiling." I know she understood what we said! A lot of you readers are not going to believe this, but I have nine relatives who have seen this occur.

Vino died when she was 14 years old due to sloppy operation and an infected incision. The whole family wept for her. She had saved my hide at least a dozen times! She would track deer, tree coon, flush pheasant and things too numerous to mention. She had been spayed at an early age, so I do not have any of her descendants. I know I will never have another dog as smart as she. However, we have several fine A.P.B.T.s now. Maybe one will turn out as well as Vino. The only place to look for that particular kind of grit, courage, loyalty and heart is in the American (Pit) Bull Terrier.

Mark Stratton with "Star"

Chapter Six

THE SOURCE

It is a wretched taste to be gratified with mediocrity when the excellent lies before us.

—Isaac D'israeli

It might be wise to preface a discussion of breeders with a brief comment on breeding techniques. One of the facts of life that breeders have eventually had to face is that when two good game dogs of different strains are crossed, a litter full of cur (i.c. nongame) pups will very likely be the result. To preserve gameness the most reputable and successful breeders have utilized inbreeding extensively and have always dreaded the time when an outcross to another strain would be necessary. In trying to find strains that would cross successfully, breeders have consistently sought out strains with a similar background. A possible explanation for this phenomenon is that gameness consists of a multiple of recessive genes. Several different combinations of these genes can produce the desired deep gameness. However, if an outcross is made to another game strain in which a different pattern of genes produces the gameness, dominant genes from each animal can block the effect of one or more of the desired recessive genes. Of course, the progeny can then be bred to each other, and a few game pups may emerge. This concept of patterns of multiple recessive genes explains why game dogs can produce curs and curs can produce game dogs (albeit rarely). In general, though, the breeder's policy is to breed game-tested stock to other proven game stock and to try to stay within a pure strain. There have been successful breedings of dogs that belonged to completely unrelated strains;

however, most of the old-time breeders attribute such happenings to sheer luck. The important genetic patterns happened, by chance, to match, or simply did not conflict.

Another point worth mentioning is that a difficult combination for a breeder to achieve is one of gameness, wrestling ability, and hard biting prowess all in one dog. Hence, most breeders concentrate on gameness alone and let the other characteristics pop up where they may.

It should also be noted here that I am only going to cover, in any depth at all, the strains that I have some personal familiarity with. Thus, many quality lines will be neglected, and it should not be considered as a reflection on their worth to be left out. It is simply a matter of my not having had first-hand knowledge of those particular strains.

Wallace's Rusty, a fine example of the Old Family Red Nose strain

First, an overview. No one really knows when these dogs first came to this country, but the great breeder William J. Lightner once told me that his grandfather raised them before the Civil War. It is quite possible that they were even here during the Revolutionary War. In any case, it is clear that dogs of this breed came from various parts of Europe, specifically Spain and Sicily. But little is known about these earliest importations, because nothing was written about them. (Books and periodicals containing information about dogs were rare in those days.) Their existence can be inferred from artwork, however. The most famous importations were from Ireland, and were generally made by the Irish themselves after they emigrated to this country. (The bulk of the Irish pit dog importations coincides or closely follows the great Irish migration that resulted from the famous potato famine.) Most of the Irish dogs were small and very closely inbred, but their gameness was proverbial—especially that of the group of strains that was known as the Old Family. The following article I wrote on the Old Family Reds (just one segment of the Old Family bloodlines) is reprinted from *Bloodlines Journal*.

THE STORY OF THE
OLD FAMILY REDS *

It has always seemed to me that the good old Pit Bull is a breed that is at once primitive and futuristic. He looks no more out of place in the ancient landscapes of 16th-century paintings than he does in the ultra-modern setting. It is beyond my capabilities to imagine an end to him, for every generation seems to supply a nucleus of hard core devotees completely committed to the breed. In any case, you can look into the murky past, and you will find it difficult to discern a beginning place for the breed, and, fortunately, the future seems to threaten no demise either.

Ours is a breed that has a definite mystique. Part of it, no doubt, stems from the fact that it is an old breed and deeply steeped in tradition. Old strains are a particularly fascinating part of this tradition, and the Old Family Red Nose is one of the better-known old strains.

The appearance of the red-nosed dogs always attracts attention, but it takes a little getting used to for some people to consider them truly beautiful. However, no one denies that they radiate "class." Characteristically, a dog of the red-nosed strain has a copper-red nose, red lips, red toe nails, and red or amber eyes. Some think the strain was bred for looks. Others consider any dog that just happens

* Appeared in the January-February, 1975 issue of *Bloodlines Journal.*

to have a red nose to be pure Old Family Red Nose. It is hoped that the following will dispel such notions.

About the middle of the last century there was a family of pit dogs in Ireland bred and fought chiefly in the counties of Cork and Kerry that were known as the "Old Family." In those days, pedigrees were privately kept and jealously guarded. Purity of the strains was emphasized to the extent that breeders hardly recognized another strain as being the same breed. For that reason all the strains were closely inbred. And whenever you have a closed genetic pool of that type, you are likely to have a slide toward the recessive traits, because the dominants, once discarded, are never recaptured. Since red is recessive to all colors but white, the "Old Family" eventually became the "Old Family Reds." When the dogs began coming to America, many were already beginning to show the red nose.

The "Old Family" dogs found their way to America mainly via immigrants. For example, Jim Corcoran came to this country to fight the world heavyweight champion John L. Sullivan, and stayed to become a Boston police-

Wallace's Red Brave, a game and rugged member of the Old Family Red Nose strain

Wallace's
"Red Rock."
13 Mo. old, 2-10-52.
Buckskin Red
Sire - Red Rube ex
Red Raven

Wallace's Red Rock, a game and rugged Old Family Red Nose specimen

man. He sent for dogs from his parents back in Ireland, and his importations and expertise as a great breeder have earned him a prominent place in American (Pit) Bull Terrier history. Many other Irish immigrants also sent back to their families to request for dogs, and the "Old Family" and related strains became firmly established in the United States.

At this point, there are several factors that are somewhat confusing to a student of the breed. For one thing, the term "family dogs" was used in two ways: It could mean a strain of dogs that was a family unto itself that was kept by a number of unrelated people in Ireland, or it could refer to a strain of dogs that was kept and preserved through the years by a family group. However, the old Family Reds seem to be of the first category. Another point that arises is that with all these importations from Ireland (and there were importations from other countries, too—including Spain), where do we get off calling our

Red Raven, the foundation bitch for Wallace's red-nosed stock. Bred by D.A. McClintock

breed the American Bull Terrier! Well. . .that's a point! The breed does not really belong to any one country or even any one era! However, I don't believe many people are in favor of changing the name of the breed even though it is not strictly an American breed. For that matter, it is not really a Bull Terrier, either! But the name American (Pit) Bull Terrier has become part of that tradition we were talking about, and I think most of us prefer to keep it as a formal name for the breed.

Back to the Old Family Reds. The first big splash made by the red noses was back around 1900 when the great breeder William J. Lightner, utilizing Old Family Red bloodlines, came up with some red-nosed dogs that really made a name for themselves. Now Lightner once told me that he did not breed for that red-nosed coloration. In fact, he did not even like it and he only put up with it because the individual dogs were of such high quality. Eventually Lightner gave up the red-nosed strain when he moved from Louisiana to Colorado, where he came up with a new strain that consisted of small dark-colored dogs with black noses. He had given up on the other strain because they were running too big for his taste and *because he didn't like the red noses.*

At this point in our story we come upon a comical, but highly-respected, figure in the personage of Dan McCoy. I have heard old-time dog men from all over the country talk about this man. Apparently, he was an itinerant fry cook and not much of a success in life judged by normal standards, but he didn't care about that. What he did care about were Pit Bulldogs, and he had a wealth of knowledge about the breed. His uncanny ability to make breedings that "clicked" made him a respected breeding consultant and a most welcome guest at any dog man's house—even if he had just dropped off a freight train!

Always with his ear to the ground regarding anything that involved APBT's, McCoy got wind of the fact that an old Frenchman in Louisiana by the name of Bourgeous had preserved the old Lightner red-nosed strain. So he and Bob Hemphill went to that area, and with the aid of Gaboon Trahan of Lafayette, they secured what was left of the dogs. McCoy took his share to the Panhandle of Texas and placed them with his associates L. C. Owens, Arthur Harvey and Buck Moon. He then played a principal role in directing the breedings that were made by these fanciers. And from this enclave came such celebrated dogs as Harvey's Red Devil and Owens (Fergusons) Centipede. Hemphill eventually kept only dogs of the red-nosed strain. According to Hemphill, it was McCoy who first started using the term "Old Family Red Nose" for the strain.

Wallace's Red Rube, part of the foundation stock of the old Wallace red-nosed line

Wallace's Red Poncho ruined his teeth as a pup, and was used as a "schooling" dog by Wallace

Another breeder who was almost synonymous with the red-nosed strain was Bob Wallace. However, Bob's basic bloodline was not pure Old Family Red Nose. But in the late 40's he was looking for the red-nosed strain in order to make an "outcross." (Bob was a scrupulously careful breeder who planned his breedings years in advance.) Unfortunately, he found that the strain was nearly gone, most of it having been ruined by careless breedings. He managed to obtain seven pure red-noses of high quality whose pedigrees he could authenticate. The strain was subsequently saved for posterity and in the 1950's became the fashionable strain in Pit Bull circles. In fact, it was Bob Wallace himself who wrote an article in 1953 called "There Is No Magic in Red Noses" in which he tried to put a damper on the overly enthusiastic claims being made by some of the admirers of the strain. No more fervent admirer of the Old Family Reds ever lived than Wallace, but he obviously felt that the strain could stand on its own merits.

Many stains have been crossed with the Old Family Reds at some time in their existence. Consequently, nearly any strain will occasionally throw a red-nosed pup. To many fanciers, these red-nosed individuals are Old Family Red Noses even though the great preponderance of their blood is that of other strains. Sometimes such individuals will fail to measure up and thereby reflect undeserved discredit on the red-nosed strain. However, as Wallace said, the red noses should not be considered invincible either. They produce their share of bad ones as well as good ones—just as all strains do.

As a strain, the Old Family Red Nose has several things going for it. First, it is renowned for its gameness. Second, some of the most reputable breeders in all Pit Bull history have contributed to the preservation and development of the strain. People like Lightner, McClintock. Menefee and Wallace, to mention just a few. Finally, as McNolty said in his *30-30 Journal* (1967) "Regardless of one's historical perspective, these old amber-eyed, red-nosed, red-toe-nailed, red-coated dogs represent some of the most significant pit bull history and tradition that stands on four legs today."

WELL-KNOWN BREEDERS

Probably the best known of all Pit Bulldog breeders was John P. Colby. He was also the center of controversy. The usual pattern of the top Irish breeders before Colby came along in the late 1800's was that they only bred to dogs within the "family" and only let dogs out to trusted friends that would safeguard the bloodlines. The dogs were considered too good for the general public, and no effort was made to popularize them. However, Colby broke the pattern in that he advertised and sold dogs and stud services to the "common" people, and he made a conscientious effort to make the breed appreciated by the public. Thus, in the eyes of many dog men he was a "peddler" (one of the worst things you can call a pit dog man). In Colby's defense, it should be mentioned that some of the great dogs of all time came from his kennels. And he was so successful at popularizing the breed that many people think of him as the fountainhead of the dogs in this country. This is not true, of course, but apparently he was a big, good-looking and robust Irishman with charm to spare. I remember seeing pictures of him with Jack Johnson and other famous sports figures, along with a favorite Pit Bull. The good he did for the breed is incalculable, and it is only fitting that he receive proper recognition.

One of the recognized great breeders of all time was D. A. McClintock, and, to my knowledge, he never matched a dog. But he was caught up in the breeding aspect of the breed, and he obviously game-tested his broodstock, as he sent out some great dogs. One of my prized possessions is a seven-generation hand-written pedigree that was made out by Mr. McClintock. Like many of the old-time breeders, he did not believe in registering his dogs, but he kept his own records in better shape than any registering body. He was instrumental in perpetuating the Old Family Red Nose strain. He also got his nephew interested in the breed, but as it ended up his nephew eventually took the show route with the breed and became one of the most influential and respected of all the Staffordshire Terrier breeders. His name was Howard M. Hadley.

I never knew Joe Corvino personally, but it is difficult not to mention him, at least in passing. He was a blacksmith in Chicago in the first half of this century, and, in addition to breeding dogs, he built some excellent treadmills. Many of these mills are still in use today and are valuable collectors' items. The Corvino strain is still intact at the time of this writing and is the preferred strain among pit dog men of all the old strains. Even pit dog people's tastes are subject to change, however, and in the near future, another fine strain is likely to be the one preferred. There is no denying, however, that Corvino founded an excellent line of dogs.

Joe Corvino with one of his charges in front of his old blacksmith shop.

One of the most colorful of the well known breeders was William J. Lightner. He was a big robust fellow who was a bareknuckle boxer in his youth and at times was employed as a bouncer. He had two constants in his life: his family and his strain of dogs. The Lightner strain was forged over a long period of time by several individuals, as Lightner's grandfather, uncle and father were all instrumental in furthering the Lightner line. When I knew Lightner, he and his wife were quite old, but both were sharp as tacks, and both of them knew these dogs inside and out. Mrs. Lightner, as a matter of fact, kept all the records and took care of all the correspondence pertaining to dogs. I once asked Mrs. Lightner, when I was a youngster, if it were not cruel to allow the dogs to fight in the pit. She answered that it was cruel all right, but not to the dogs, for fighting was the very breath of life to them because of their breeding. But it was cruel to the people because it was hard not to get especially attached to your best dog, the very one likely to be matched, and sometimes they were lost. I never knew a more devoted couple than the Lightners, so, naturally, it was quite a blow to the old man when his wife preceded him in death. He carried on courageously, however, but kept a fresh flower in front of her picture every day until his own death. His contribution to the breed includes the Old Family Red Nose strain and the modern-day Lightner strain, consisting pretty much of small, variable-colored dogs. One of the great mysteries of Pit Bull history was where this second strain came from. As far as I know, no one ever found out!

The breeder I knew best was R. F. Wallace, and I have to admit to a definite prejudice in his behalf. Perhaps the best I can do here is to reprint an article I wrote for *Bloodlines Journal.*

BOB WALLACE – BREEDER PAR EXCELLENCE [*]

Most devotees of the American (Pit) Bull Terrier are aware that the breed is made up of a number of separate strains. As is the case with Foxhounds, quality strains carry the name of their originator. This is a nice form of

[*] Appeared in the July-August, 1974 issue of *Bloodlines Journal.*

recognition for the breeder, but, ironically, full acceptance of a strain often does not come until long after the death of its founder. Thus the strains of Colby and Lightner are almost unassailable today because of the general recognition that they have produced or contained their share of good dogs. Yet when I was a boy there was considerable controversy about the worth of these two lines. Breeders

Bob Wallace, "The Old Master"

are the creative element within the hobby, and as such, they and their product are always subject to criticism. Consequently, just as we need distance from a mountain range to see which mountain is the tallest, we need time to see the breeders of a given era in true perspective. In

Wallace's Penny, the foundation bitch of what was to become the Wallace bloodline

my opinion, Bob Wallace will some day be acknowledged as the greatest breeder of his era.

I was only 17 years old when I first met Bob, and I was immediately afflicted with a strong case of hero worship. Here, I thought, was a model for all pit dog men! (Bob is over 70 years old now and a thousand miles away, yet I can almost hear him laughing at such nonsense as I write these words!) I can't claim any degree of objectivity in writing about Bob or his dogs, for he has been a lifelong friend, and I'm not sure I ever lost that case of hero worship. Still, it might be interesting to the reader to know of some of his qualities and of his work with this great breed.

To begin with, Bob was an impressive person in his own right. He had been a football player and boxer in his youth, yet he was educated and articulate. He loved all dogs, but he was completely dedicated to the American (Pit) Bull Terrier. His dogs were impressive, but so was the way he kept them. He had pens and kennel runs for puppies and females in whelp, but he was convinced that the best way to keep adult kennel dogs of this breed was to keep them chained to a trolley on a cable. It was his opinion that the dogs were more active on cables than in pens or kennel runs. Since Bob had purchased a beautiful seven-acre country place, the dogs had lots of room to run (on their cables). To sum up my feelings of my first visit to the Wallace home, it was a beautiful place that "showcased" some very fine-looking dogs. Bob and his lovely wife Doris were concerned and gracious people. It is not difficult to understand why a homesick young paratrooper would be smitten by these fine folks. But the fact that they took me in, welcomed me on my many (and often impromptu) visits and truly made me feel that their home was my "home-away-from-home" is an indication of their quality and sensitivity.

Somehow, in spite of all my visits, I never met Bob's father, but I understand he was quite a sportsman and that he raised coonhounds. But when Bob was only five years old he received the gift of a Pit Bull pup, and from that time on he was a "Bulldog" man!

Wallace's Tonoy, one of the dogs on which the renowned Wallace line was bred

The story of how Bob began to build his own strain of dogs would be an article by itself; consequently, the details will be covered in a later issue. For now, it is sufficient to say that Bob bred his share of good ones. Oddly enough, most people associate the Wallace bloodlines with the "Old Family Red Nose" strain. The fact is that the old Wallace dogs were only part red nose, and later on in his career, Bob secured the red nose strain and kept it pure to utilize for "outcrossing" his own strain into.

It is difficult for any breeder—especially one whose career was as long as Wallace's—to select his "best dog". But, certainly one of the best had to be Wallaces King Cotton. It was not just that he won the biggest-monied pit contest of his time, nor even that his opponent had virtually annihilated four fine dogs before he met King (who stopped him in an hour and 38 minutes). Rather, it was that he was such an all-around good dog—well built, good looking, intelligent—and he had the uncanny ability to solve any dog's fighting style and turn it against him. King was the son of Wallaces Toney, a dog that was famous for having made one of the gamest "scratches" of all time, and a grandson of Wallaces Searcy Jeff, who was generally considered the best pit dog of his time. King's picture graced Bob's stationery for years, and his blood runs strong in all the pure presentday Wallace dogs.

King was just one of many fine dogs I observed when I first visited the Wallaces, but I was amazed that his kennels also contained a couple of Cocker Spaniel-type mongrels. As it turned out, Bob Wallace was a true dog lover, and he just could not resist an injured or abandoned dog. He invariably picked them up, brought them home, nursed them back to health and found homes for them. Those that he was unable to find homes for remained in his kennels until he *could* find homes for them!

It may seem strange to some that a downright maudlin dog lover such as Wallace could be a pit dog man. I think he had trouble understanding that himself. My own belief is that he simply loved the breed so much that he was determined to do his part to maintain and improve the gameness that is the trademark of the American (Pit) Bull Terrier. That he more than succeeded is evident not only from the many fine dogs that he produced throughout the years but also from the high regard—and high prices!—that his strain commands today. Success was not attained without considerable sacrifice and complete dedication on the part of both Bob and Doris Wallace. All pit bull fanciers owe them a debt, for they have improved the breed by the addition of a fine strain.

One of those rare successful father-and-son teams is composed of Lawrence McCaw and his son Bruce, and let there be no mistake about it, this is a team that has produced results! The McCaws are among the most serious students of the breed I have ever known. Any literature pertaining to the dogs in any way whatsoever is stored away in their special dog library. Before any breeding is made, the ancestry of the dogs is thoroughly researched and analyzed. Stringent standards have paid off in the formation of a high-quality strain that the McCaws call the Going Light line. Although they have their own qual-

Larry McCaw and Barney

97

Floyd Boudreaux with "Ox"

ity strain, it is to their credit to note that they have been instrumental in the preservation of other high-quality lines, such as the Jim Williams red-nosed line. The McCaws have also worked to attempt the salvation of a quality segment of the Colby line. Larry and Bruce seem to have a method of making a success out of any undertaking, whether business or hobby, so it should come as no surprise that they have succeeded so well with the dogs. Some of their all-time great dogs have been Going Light Barney, Going Light Babe, Going Light Joe and Going Light Feather.

Floyd Boudreaux is another of those breeders who inherited his interest in the dogs, as well as the dogs themselves, from his father. His line has been kept pure, with very few outcrosses. Mr. Boudreaux is one of the most highly respected of all the modern breeders, both for the quality of the dogs and for his own personal qualities. This

Champion Stubblefield's Buddy, an easy-going powerhouse!

man has truly "lived" these dogs all his life and has made many valuable contributions to the breed, both in breeding stock and in personal service.

It is with a sense of frustration that I end this chapter, for while its purpose, to provide just a glimpse of some of the people that have founded recognized strains, has been fulfilled, I still have much I would like to tell. For example, I would like to give the full story of Ham Morris of Louisville, Kentucky, who was a genius with animals other than dogs. When I met him in 1950, he had race horses, too, and had a horse that had been trained to drive a modified car. No, I'm not kidding—in fact, *Life* magazine ran a story on the animal! Then there was the dog trainer who trained Labrador Retrievers for a living but raised Pit Bulls as his hobby. In short, I may have met Pit Bull fanciers, on occasion, that I didn't especially like, but none of them was ever dull!

Chapter Seven

SOME FAMOUS DOGS

Tiger! Tiger! burning bright
In the forests of the night,
What immortal hand or eye
Could frame thy fearful symmetry?

—William Blake

I have often been amused by Staffordshire or Bull Terrier people as I listened to them debate about the physical traits that make for a top fighting dog. The irony is that such people are involved in serious debate about something they usually know absolutely nothing about. Thus they tend to overemphasize physical characteristics that make a dog *look* tough, such as a large head or a heavily-built or stocky body. Most show people tend to go to extremes in conformation, and we thereby get ridiculously straight pasterns, rear legs locked forward, and tight little compact feet. I recall a show person looking in horror at a picture of "Crosspatch" (the winner of a top field trial for bird dogs) and exclaiming how cowhocked the dog was. Well. . .performance is proof of the pudding, and if this person had ever seen a bird dog field trial, she would know that Crosspatch had to have strength, endurance and mobility in his hindquarters in order to win that field trial! So don't talk to us about conformation—especially in view of the fact that conformation people (i.e. show dog people) bear the brunt of the blame for the cruel and dreaded disease called hip dysplasia. In any case, this chapter is intended to demonstrate the degrees of physical variation in the very top dogs that have come along in the last sixty years.

Unfortunately, the selections here have been necessarily limited by my own knowledge and the availability of pictures. It grieves me to leave out such proven dogs as Cincinnati Paddy and White Rock, but one was just too far back in time, and I was unable to obtain pictures of the other. To be perfectly candid, though, this chapter is intended to give a sampling of what good dogs are like more than it is to give recognition to deserving dogs. The arrangement is in chronological order, with no attempt to rank one of these dogs above another.

COLBY'S PINSCHER: 72 pounds; 1910

Pinscher's pit record is vague, and for that reason he has been a subject of some controversy. However, Colby always referred to him as one of his alltime great dogs, and others who were in the area during Pinscher's heyday confirm his greatness. He apparently was game and a killing punisher. Most of our dogs have him in their pedigrees if we trace them back far enough. For those who wonder about the name, there were no Dobermans back in those days, and *pinscher* was the German word for "terrier." Unfortunately, that leaves us with another mystery: why would an

Colby's Pinscher

Harry Clark
with Kager

Irishman give the German name for terrier to a box-headed dog like Pinscher?

ARMITAGES KAGER: 47 pounds; 1919

Kager was bred by John P. Colby, and, as a matter of fact, was a descendant of Colby's Pinscher. That he was a

**Earl Tudor
with Black Jack**

good pit dog is attested to by the fact that both George Armitage and Harry Clark proclaimed him the greatest dog they had ever seen. According to legend, Kager was once the pet of a driver of a whisky wagon and rode on the wagon everywhere with his master; he thus was appropriately named "Whisky." Colby got the dog back when his master became a policeman and no longer had time for the dog. He was subsequently sold to Armitage, who changed his name to Kager and matched him under that name. Later Harry Clark purchased Kager but fought him under the name of Clark's Tramp. Apparently, most of the breedings made to Kager were made while Clark owned him, as "Clark's Tramp" is the only way I have seen him appear on a pedigree.

TUDORS BLACK JACK: 49 pounds; 1920

Earl Tudor always named Black Jack as the finest dog he had ever seen. Apparently, the dog was no slouch, as he was many times matched with dogs much heavier than he was, and he always won. As a matter of fact, he was open to whatever was available at any weight. Unfortunately, not much is known about the breeding on this dog, but the word I have is that he was Delihant on the top side and Swineford on his dam's side. That is only hearsay, but his matches are well substantiated, and everyone whom I ever knew who saw him proclaimed him the best!

SEARCY JEFF: 39 pounds; 1940

This dog was proclaimed the best they had ever seen by both Bob Wallace and Bob Hemphill. Jeff was a killing punisher that would nearly bite a dog's head right off. Like most bone-crushing pit aces, Jeff's deep gameness was questioned by dog men. (Since Jeff would render a dog helpless in a matter of minutes, his matches never went very long, and his gameness was thus never proved before the public.) However, after his teeth were ruined from fighting rocks, Jeff was purchased by Bob Wallace (a king's ransom couldn't have got him before that time). Since Wallace planned to base his entire strain of dogs on Jeff, he felt it absolutely necessary to game-test him. He used three different dogs in turn on Jeff, and the dog took it all and begged for more!

King
Cotton

Wallace's
Searcy
Jeff

WALLACES KING COTTON: 39 pounds; 1950

King has already been discussed to some extent under
the section on breeders, but he's worth coming back to.
Here was a dog that was the epitome of everything that is
good about the American Pit Bull Terrier. It was my pleasure to have been acquainted with this particular animal,
and I would give a pretty penny to have one like him. He
was a fine-looking dog, and, like so many other Pit Bulls,
he had an ideal disposition and a real happy-go-lucky attitude. As a pit dog, he was renowned because of his
nearly unbelievable ability. His contest against Corvinos
Blackie "made" his reputation. Most pit dog men were not
overly fond of the Blackie dog, as he was a "maneater,"
and it is part of the pit dog man's credo that a mean dog is
never dead game. Blackie was putting this idea to a severe
test, however, as he had beaten four fine dogs in a row! At
the match between Blackie and King Cotton, the pit was
wired in to protect the spectators from Blackie, and the referee carried a club to protect the men in the pit—just in
case! Three handlers with three leashes brought the muz-
zled animal into the pit. King dominated the fight from

start to finish, and Blackie refused to scratch at the hour and thirty-one minute mark. Thus, King Cotton became an instant hero by beating a very unpopular dog that no one had seemed able to stop.

GOOFY: 49 pounds; 1960

Here was a dog that was living proof that a dog did not have to look strong to be a veritable powerhouse! In fact, Lou Johnston told me that he went out of his way before a match to let the other side see Goofy, and thus was able to drive up the odds. But Goofy was a phenomenal fighting dog with tremendous strength and biting ability. In addition, he was an extremely intelligent and ring-wise dog who had a vast repertoire of holds and manuevers. Goofy lived to a ripe old age in the hands of Lou Johnston, and there are many dog men around who list him as the greatest that they have ever seen.

GOING LIGHT BARNEY: 39 pounds; 1970

Since my own information on Barney is somewhat limited, I have chosen to reprint an article on him here that originally appeared in *Sporting Dog Journal.*

Johnston's Goofy

PORTRAIT OF AN ACE *
By: Red Rover

Although pit dog men vary in occupations, education, politics and even in our ideas about the dogs, I would venture to say that one thing we do have in common is the dream of some day owning an "Ace." Some of the lucky ones amongst us have already attained this dream, perhaps more than once. But generally speaking, an "ace" is a once-in-a-lifetime dog. He is a dog that can whip anything his own weight and make it look easy. In fact, some of the better ones didn't even have to be matched to weight.

The pattern of public reaction to an ace is a familiar one and fairly predictable. While most fanciers are quick with their acclaim, there is always a hardcore group of diehards and skeptics. The usual comment is that the dog is a cur (albeit a "stiff cur"), and that soon a dog will come along that will make him show his true colors. Eventually, credit is grudgingly given, although it may not be until long after the dog has died!

Actually, some of the old-timers have a right to be suspicious of the rough, devastating type of Bulldog that wins by rendering his opponent helpless in a matter of minutes. Experienced breeders are only too aware of how difficult it is to get all the desirable components—hard bite, gameness, good wrestling ability and pit intelligence—in one dog. More often than not, if we get a hardbiting, rough dog, he turns out not to be game. If we get a deeply game dog, he seemingly can't bite through a paper bag! These qualities are not mutually exclusive, as used to be argued by some dog men, but they are statistically difficult to obtain in one dog.

However, an ace is more than just all the qualities of a good pit dog combined in one dog. Usually a phenomenal ability of some kind is also involved. Thus we have Owens Tanner, a dog that would shake so hard he banged his opponent's head on the ground, completely disorienting him. Or Wallaces Searcy Jeff, who would feed an opponent his

* Appeared in the July-August, 1975 issue of *Sporting Dog Journal.*

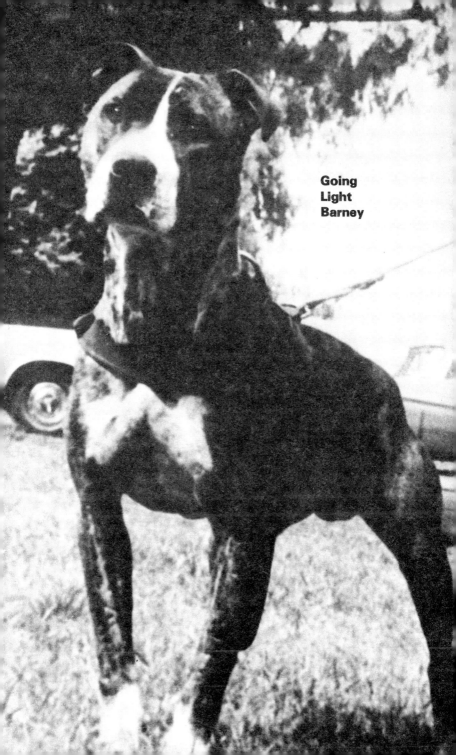

**Going
Light
Barney**

right front leg, then practically bite his head right off! Or Tudors Black Jack, a Colby-bred dog who killed quality opponents that outweighed him by a considerable amount.

Most of us have logged in considerable time mooning over pictures of such dogs, wishing we had a time machine to go back and get them! However, it only stands to reason that there is an ace or two in our midst right now—especially if we take into account the theory of large numbers. There are more people now and more pit dog men—hence, more pit dogs. We would therefore expect that there would be more good dogs, which, I think, there are. (Also, unfortunately, more bad ones!) I'm sure everybody has his

Going Light Babe, litter sister to Barney

own idea of a dog that might be our generation's ace. My own candidate is Going Light Barney.

Barney is an eight-time winner, but, more than that, he is an eight-time winner that has been open to the world and has had run at him the finest dogs that were available. Because of his tremendous punishing power, many of Barney's matches have been short. But because of the quality of his opponents, Barney has gone the distance a number of times, and, on such occasions he has exhibited excellent ring generalship, pacing himself, coasting, waiting for the proper moment, then really pouring on the heat!

As for his fighting style, he is an ear dog *par excellence,* but he has tremendous adaptability. In fact, he is one of those rare dogs that have the uncanny ability to solve any dog's fighting style and turn it against him. His wrestling ability and biting power are nothing short of phenomenal. His scratches are spectacular, but they have not been frequent, as, again because of the quality of his opponents, there have been very few turns in any of his contests.

Barney was bred by Lawrence McCaw and his son Bruce, utilizing an old Corvino-bred stud dog owned by Morrie Rootberg and a bitch strong in the blood of Rascal and the fabulous Goofy (owned by Lou Johnston). In the seven years that they have owned Barney, Larry and Bruce have utilized hardnosed selectivity and saturation breeding techniques to found a bloodline based on Barney that they call the "Going Light" strain. Both men are completely committed to Bulldogs and are highly respected among pit dog men.

It may seem as though praise of Barney has been too lavish and overdrawn, but, remember, we are dealing with an ace here, and it is sometimes difficult to communicate just how much such a dog stands out. An incident involving Barney's schooling may make the point. Larry and Bruce were involved in game-testing Barney and w' nted to be sure he could take it. The only hitch was that 'e had such uncanny ability to counter a dog's fighting style that Barney didn't have to take much—even when larger dogs were put on him. After trying a number of different dogs with different fighting styles on Barney, all to no avail, one of the handlers suddenly had an idea. "Maybe," he said, "if we tied Barney up, the other dogs could do something with him!"

The idea, of course, was dismissed as ridiculous. But the fact that it could even be suggested in earnest is an indication of just how complete was Barney's dominance!

Lehman's Jet

Chapter Eight

SOME QUESTIONS AND ANSWERS

Old people like to give good advice, as solace for no longer being able to provide bad examples.
                                    —François, Duc De La Rochefoucauld

The following questions were sent to *Bloodlines Journal* and were answered by me in a column called "Pit Bull Particulars." They are reprinted here in the hope that they will be of some interest to the reader.

Question: *"Please write on what happens when you breed to show standards." (Mrs. Marilyn Rivera, Lakewood, California.)*

Answer: (Many thanks for your nice letter and the picture of your fine-looking dog.) I don't wish to discourage those groups who have organized for the purpose of showing their dogs—especially since, as I understand it, the purpose of the shows is not so much that of competition, but rather, to provide public exposure for the breed. Still, it is not difficult to visualize the competition within the show eventually becoming the main interest of the groups involved. And, to be perfectly candid, I must admit that breeding to a show standard has a tendency to ruin the *performance* breeds. For that reason, bird dog people have established a separate registry for their dogs—just to make sure that none of the A.K.C. show stock gets mixed up with theirs. Border Collie people have their own registry for the same reason. Breeders of coonhounds register their dogs with the U.K.C. and maintain strict control over their breed by making certain a dog does not become a bench champion until he has demonstrated hunting ability. Field trial Beagle people shy away from show stock like poison, claiming that show Beagles will not even *chase* a rabbit, let alone trail one.

It seems to me that what *Bloodlines* has done is to provide a forum for the people who like the APBT as a breed but do not care for the pit contests. Even though many owners of the breed abhor pit contests, most of them still want a game dog. Fortunately, the U.K.C. did not "close off" the game strains, as did the A.K.C. For that reason, it might be possible for the APBT to remain game even though it were being shown in U.K.C. sponsored shows— as long as owners bred only to dogs that were proven game. Still, I am inclined to ally myself with those who say "Forget the shows!" The famous veterinarian Leon Whitney once told of how his breed, the working Bloodhound, was ruined by show people—and it is sober reading!

Question: *"Many subscribers to* Bloodlines *are young people who haven't had a chance to see even pictures of some of the old-time great pit dogs. Could extracts from old* Bloodlines *be put into future editions?" (Walter Scott, Cleveland, Ohio.)*

Answer: Unfortunately, no picture file has been kept. However, it is my intention to ferret out old-time pictures from some "old-time" friends and to get as many as possible published. Truly, those great old dogs deserve to be immortalized!

Question: *"Where can I obtain more information about the Pit Bull? Are there any current books in publication on the APBT or Staffordshire, or any other magazines or journals a person can subscribe to?" (Mr. & Mrs. Terry L. Flory, Walnut Springs, Texas.)*

Question: *"I am in search of some books on this outstanding breed. I have searched high and low and still am unable to find any. If you are able to tell me where I may obtain books on this subject, it will be much appreciated." (Victor Fong, Honolulu, Hawaii).*

"Tucker," son of
Going Light Jim

Davis' Peg proves
that a Pit Bull can fit
in with any room
decor!

Going
Light
Katie

Answer: There are several books that were written on the breed, but they have been written mostly from the pit dog point of view. The following is an annotated list:

Armitage, George; *Thirty Years with Fighting Dogs,* Washington, D.C., 1935. This book is out of print, but a friend of mine found a copy at a used book store. Advice, especially on feeding, is out-of-date and much of the writing is biased, but the book, with its many pictures, should prove useful and fascinating to the student of the breed.

Colby, J. L.; *The American Pit Bull* Terrier, Sacramento, California, 1936. This little book was written by one of John P. Colby's sons and is well worth having—if you can find a copy!

Denlinger, Milo G; *The Complete Staffordshire Terrier or PitBull,* Washington, D.C., 1948. This book is composed of a "hash" of writings lifted from old *Bloodlines,* Staffordshire Bull Terrier books, and other sources. The writings are usually not separated or identified; consequently, this book has added to the confusion about the breed. In spite of this fault, it is a favorite of mine and I recommend it. (It is out of print but more easily found than the others. Look in old pet stores that carry books, old book stores, etc.)

Hanna, L.B., *Memories of the Pit Bull Terrier and his Master,* New York, 1926. This book, written long ago, was reprinted in 1955, but is once again out of print. Most old books like this are chiefly valued as a collector's item and for the pictures they contain.

Ormsby, C.A.; *The Staffordshire Terrier,* New York, 1956. This is the best of the "Staff" books in my opinion. It has a short section on history, a story about "Pete" (the "Our Gang" movie dog), and the rest is pretty much about show dogs.

The following are fiction stories about the Pit Bull that I have run across in my "researches".

Foote, John Tantor; *Allegheny.* (A Pit Bull pup, slated for death in the Allegheny River because of a ruined leg, is saved by a physician and later repays his benefactor by saving his son's life when he is attacked by a rabid Great Dane.)

Foote, John Tantor; *Trubs Diary*. (A fanciful but amusing story told in the dog's own words! A drunken playboy buys a Pit Bull pup while "under the influence" for his old maid aunt and guardian. When he sobers up, all he remembers is that the kennel man told him that the dog's middle name would be trouble. This is truly the funniest dog story I've ever read, and it will have you howling and holding your sides!)

Kirk, R. G.; *White Monarch and the Gas House Pup*. (A 28 pound Pit Bull is matched against a 60 pound Bulldog. The rich and snobbish people are supporting the Bulldog, while the poor working people are depending on the pit bull to win.)

Thurber, James; *A Portrait of Rex*. (The famous author and former editor of the *New Yorker* tells some true stories about his boyhood pal, an "American Bull Terrier"!)

Question: *Since a Bullmastiff is supposedly a cross between a Bulldog and a Mastiff, can such a cross be made now and registered as purebreds?*

John E. Langford
Carthage, Texas

Answer: No, for two reasons. First, crossbreedings rarely produce a uniform litter; it takes generations of subsequent selective breeding to accomplish this. Second, most breed histories are suspect (although the Bullmastiff's is probably correct). For example, the commonly-accepted version of our breed's history was probably constructed from writings done on the history of the (English) Bull Terrier.

Question: *1. What is meant by a "jugheaded" Pit Bull? by a "shovelheaded" Pit Bull?*
2. A special article explaining the historical orgins and salient characteristics of the many bloodlines (Colby, Wallace, Tudor, etc.) would be very interesting and most informative to newcomers to the breed, like myself.

Joseph LaGuerra
Roslyn Heights, NY

Jone's Tuffy

Wise's Sandy

Tiger
Jack

Answer: A "jug-headed" dog is usually just a heavy-headed dog. "Shovel-headed" is the normal Pit Bull head, tapering in gently toward the snout. In good time, I hope to come up with articles on the major strains and stories on some of the most important breeders. Of the strains you mention, Colby is a widely-dispersed strain and generally considered of high quality (although all strains have their critics!) The Wallace line is less widely dispersed, but it is an important and high-quality strain. (The reasons the Wallace line is not widely dispersed is that Wallace, as a matter of principle, never sold his dogs.) There is no Tudor strain in the sense of pure line, as Tudor himself, I think, would be the first to point out, as he never claimed to be a breeder. However, he was probably associated with more good dogs than any other man in Pit Bull history. It must be said that although he never started a strain, some great dogs came from breedings he made.

Question: *I'm the owner of an all-white male Pit Bull. Not long ago a friend picked me up and drove me to a place where there was something he said he had to show me. We pulled into a gas station, and there I found an all-white female dog exactly the same size and conformation as my dog. I tried to talk the owner into breeding white Pit Bulls, but he wouldn't hear of it because, though he thought they looked alike and had similar traits (his dog had killed a 280-pound wild boar in Argentina), his was an "Argentinian Dogo" and he wouldn't breed his dog with anything that didn't have "Dogo" papers. Now, I had thought that I knew my Pit Bulls fairly well, so my question is: what in the world is a Dogo? He says in Argentina they are all white. Perhaps it is another name for the same breed?*

Another brief question I have really wanted answered is how good are these "Bandogs" that are popping up? They are a Pit Bull-Italian Bull cross. I'm not a dog fighter, but I am curious as to how well a pure Pit Bull "stacks up" with them.

Carl Semencic
Jackson Hts., NY

119

Answer: Countless dogs of our breed have been sent to South America ostensibly for the control of predatory animals. I think it would be unrealistic to believe that the breed would continue to be known by the name American (Pit) Bull Terrier. Also, it is perfectly logical that certain variations of the breed would come about—just as the Old Family Red Nose did in this country.

As for the Italian Bandog, that particular term (which used to mean bound dog or chain dog) was used for the old Mastiff or Bulldog centuries ago. I would assume that this, too, is a variation of our breed.

There are other fighting dogs found throughout the world. I have received some feedback from Pit Bull fanciers who have viewed them in their own country, and the usual comment is, "If these dogs just had a little more A.P.B.T. bred into them, they might not be too bad"! Of course, we have to allow for prejudice on the part of the observers, but from all evidence I have been able to obtain, the A.P.B.T. reigns supreme at his own game—regardless of weight! That doesn't mean that the old adage "A good big man can always beat a good little man" has been disproved by the Pit Bull. That adage still applies. It is just that the A.P.B.T. is a *very good* "little man"!

Question: *What is the best exercise to build up the neck portion of the American (Pit) Bull Terrier and his chest?*

Norman R. Gonsalves
Lihue, Hawaii

Answer: Humans, if sufficiently motivated, are able to compensate for their lack of heredity by indulging in many hours of general body-building exercises. However, our dogs are bred to be well built, and exercises to increase the bulk of the muscles are not needed. Anyway, some of the best dogs have not had gigantic musculature. (Obviously, coordination and muscle quality are overriding considerations here.) However, it certainly does a dog no harm to work a hide, and retrieving two-by-fours (or larger) not only builds the dog's neck and chest, but also never fails to amuse and impress friends. Start out by teaching your dog

A Pit Bull retrieving a "stick"

to retrieve a stick, then gradually increase the size of the "stick." Another variation of this is to start out with a small bicycle tire and later use a full-size automobile tire. The famous author James Thurber once said of his A.P.B.T. "that he would have retrieved a grand piano if they could only have found a way to throw it for him"! In any case, most Pit Bulls love to fetch, and the bigger the "stick," the better!

Question: *Does any other dog compare with the A(P)BT for gameness, grit and aggressiveness (e.g. Mastiffs, Bullmastiffs, Boxers, Bull Terriers, etc)?*

John E. Langford
Carthage, Texas

Answer: No. None of them even comes close!

Question: *Is it true that some American (Pit) Bull Terriers are being destroyed by animal control shelters rather than being offered out for adoption as pets?*

John Murray
Chicago, IL

Answer: In at least one Southern California city, an official of an animal control center took it upon himself to establish that policy. This self-appointed "expert" on the A.P.B.T. based his policy on two assumptions: (1) that it was the best thing for the breed and (2) that American (Pit) Bull Terriers are dangerous to other animals. Well...with "friends" like that, the A.P.B.T. doesn't need any enemies! As for the breed being a danger to other animals, some of them are, but so what! You just don't let them run loose, that's all! Our official would be more properly concerned with the countless dogs that are a danger to people, particularly small children. Luckily, this discussion is somewhat academic. For, to their credit, the local newspapers raised such a fuss that the official involved was pressured to drop his ill-considered plan!

Question: *Why do you feel that the A.P.B.T. and the Staffordshire Bull Terrier are not the same breed–even though they have a similar appearance?*

J. Heffner
West Germany

Answer: First of all, to the practiced eye of anyone thoroughly familiar with the breeds, the resemblance is not even close. You might have to see the dogs in person, though, to appreciate the difference. However, the American Staffordshire Terrier (a different breed) and the American (Pit) Bull Terrier are very close in appearance, and it takes a truly practiced eye to see the difference. The situation we have here is one in which two breeds (the Staffordshire Bull Terrier and the American Staffordshire Terrier) are in the process of evolving away from the parent stock (the American (Pit) Bull Terrier). In any case, the real difference is something that can't be seen. That is that the A.P.B.T. is generally game, whereas the Staffordshire Bull Terrier and the American Staffordshire Terrier have lost this hard-to-keep trait.

Three breeds that are often confused. From left to right: a Staffordshire Bull Terrier, an American Staffordshire Terrier, and an American Pit Bull Terrier.

Question: *If the American (Pit) Bull Terrier is not a cross of the "brachycephalic" Bulldog and a terrier, why are some A.P.B.T.s born with kinky tails and an undershot jaw? I agree with your ideas, but was wondering about how you explain these "throwbacks.*

Henry Kranz
Syracuse, N.Y.

Answer: The term "throwback" can be a very misleading term. For example, if, as frequently happens, an American (Pit) Bull Terrier is born with a long head, we don't say that he is a "throwback" to the Collie! The only reason we are inclined to call anything a throwback to the old-type brachycephalic Bulldog is that the idea that our breed was manufactured by a cross with that breed has been incul-

The proper type of kennel run for a Pit Bull. It is roomy and only has cement around the edges.

cated into us. In other words, the term "throwback" is based on an unwarranted assumption. The truth is that there is natural variation in all breeds. Even hounds and Border Collies occasionally have kinky tails and crooked legs. Although I have seen such variation in those breeds, I have never heard anyone try to characterize it as a "throwback" to the old Bulldog!

Question: *Are American (Pit) Bull Terriers always kept on a chain, and doesn't it make them mean?*

Joe Lober
Oil City, PA

Answer: The A.P.B.T. is often kept on a chain but not always. The problem is that these dogs are capable of leaping or climbing tall fences. Since it is essential that the Pit Bull not run loose (and, incidentally, it is contrary to law in most cities and counties to allow any dog to run loose!), a fool-proof method of keeping him confined is needed. A chain is an economical way to do it. It most assuredly does not make a dog mean. The idea that a chain makes a dog mean is a public misconception that confuses cause with effect. If a dog is mean, he is more likely to be chained; hence, more dogs that are chained are mean—but the chains didn't make them that way. Another phenomenon at work here is that many dogs are more likely to make threat displays (bluff) on a chain—just as they are through a fence. For that reason, they might appear mean on a chain (just as they would in a kennel run). In any case, using a chain to confine a Pit Bull is reasonable and humane. Care must be taken, however, that there are no obstacles that the dog can jump over or he can end up hanging himself. In my opinion, the chain-on-a-cabletrolley hookup is superior even to kennel runs. Incidentally, it should be noted that some of the finest bird dogs in the world are kept on chains. The main reason show people utilize kennel runs rather than chains is that the heavy collar may rub off some of the hair on the neck or cause it

Top view of some excellent kennel runs

to grow in such a manner that the dog may not look at his absolute best in the show ring.

Question: *I have seen American (Pit) Bull Terriers 70, 80, and 90 pounds. I've also heard that they come as large as 100 pounds. In view of the fact that the A.P.B.T. was directly descended from the Staffordshire Bull Terrier of England, a breed which seldom goes over 40 pounds, how did this excess size come about?*

Daniel's Broke Tail

Marvin Parker
Queens, N.Y.

Answer: Well, first of all, I certainly challenge the assumption that the A.P.B.T. is a descendant of the Staffordshire Bull Terrier, although this curious idea has certainly been circulated in print. Rather the Staffordshire Bull Terrier has evolved from the A.P.B.T. To be more specific, the Staffordshire Bull Terrier has evolved from pit dog stock of the British Isles. The American (Pit) Bull Terrier today is identical to that stock of over a hundred years ago, whereas the Staffordshire Bull Terrier, which was recog-

"Willie" demonstrates the famous Pit Bull "grin"!

nized as a breed in 1935, is not (being more stockily built, having a shorter and more snipy muzzle, etc.). (It is useful here to keep in mind that show dogs tend to change appearance in accordance with the style of the moment. Also, there is a tendency to emphasize the distinguishing features of a breed to the extent that the dogs become virtual caricatures of their progenitors.) While the A.P.B.T. is an amalgamation of pit stock from the British Isles, Spain and Sicily, even if that were not the case, we should not be surprised at the occasional large dogs that turn up. Even some of the small-type Irish dogs that were imported begat large individuals, such as Colby's Pinscher (72 pounds). The fact is that variety of size is a traditional feature of the American (Pit) Bull Terrier breed (and, I think, a desirable one).

Question: *Rumors are flying that United Kennel Club is registering Staffordshire Bull Terriers and Bull Terriers as*

Concho's Tiger Babe

American (Pit) Bull Terriers. If this is so, won't that ruin our dogs?

Marilyn Rivera
Lakewood, Ca

Answer: I have been assured by Mr. Miller (president of the United Kennel Club) that the U.K.C. will not knowingly register any other breed under the name American (Pit) Bull Terrier. Apparently, the rumors began from a misinterpretation of remarks Mr. Miller made about the United Kennel Club's practice of registering American Staffordshire Terriers as A.P.B.T.s. If I were in charge, I would even eliminate that; however, I can see his point, since some Staffs have been dual-registered for years (and so have some Pit Bulls).

Question: *Recently, I compared the current U.K.C. American (Pit) Bull Terrier Standard with an old one appearing in the July 1940 issue of* Bloodlines. *The significant differences between the two, and the personal preferences of various breeders, set me wondering about the discrepancies encountered. The conformation standard for the A.P.B.T. must be functionally grounded because this is unquestionably a performance breed; this much I know. Consequently, the criterion for choosing between different anatomical specifications must be: What worked best in the pit? From this historical perspective, perhaps you could re-*

solve or at least clarify the following conflicting descriptions:

(1) Head: The old standard calls for a "wedgelike" shape while the new one specified "bricklike." In a previous letter I asked you what is meant by a "shovel-headed" Pit Bull. Your answer was that this expression refers to "the normal Pit Bull head, tapering in gently toward the snout." In other words, your description coincides with the old specification. Most breeders agree. Why, then, was the standard changed? Which is preferable, in light of my introductory remarks?

(2) Muzzle: The old standard calls for one of "medium" length with a "distinct stop"; the new one prefers a muzzle that is "deep," and no mention of a stop is made. Which is preferable?

(3) Chest & Forelegs: The old standard refers to a chest that is "deep and broad" It also specifies "forelegs of

King's Lewis, a black and tan inbred pup from Bruno-Heinzl bloodlines

considerable width to give the appearance of muscularity." It further states that there be "no bend in the forelegs." The new one calls for a chest that is "deep, but not too broad." The new one is silent on the width of the forelegs, but it implicitly calls for forelegs that are closer together; they must conform to a not "too broad" chest. The new standard does not specifically outlaw or discourage the breeding of dogs with bowed or bent forelegs. Which is preferable?

(4) Neck: The old standard mentions a neck of "medium" length. The new one is silent on this point. What should the neck length be?

(5) Tail: The old standard specifies that it is "definitely not be docked." No such prohibition is made in the new. Is either style acceptable?

(6) Nose: The old standard does not mention color, but the

Petronelli's Sugar

new one states that "black is preferred." Why are the rednosed *Pit Bulls* discriminated against?

(7) *Size:* No mention of size is made in either standard. However, the *A.K.C. standard for the American Staffordshire Terrier specifies a height of 17-18 inches for the female and 18-19 inches for the male. Would you like to hold Pit Bulls to this height range?*

(8) *Weight: The old standard gives a range of 30-60 lbs. for females and 40-70 lbs. for males. The new one prefers females 30-50 lbs. and males 35-60 lbs. You stated in the May-June 1975 issue of* Bloodlines *that "a good big man can always beat a good little man." Among boxers (the human variety), this is true up to a limiting optimal weight beyond which decreasing speed and agility offset any increase in power that might accompany the higher weight. What is the analogous optimal weight for a Pit Bull? In other words, at what weights is a pit dog superior to all other pit dogs either lighter of heavier than it, assuming all those being chosen from are Champions (the best) in their respective weight divisions? It seems reasonable that the optimal weight, whatever it is, should form the basis for establishing the upper and lower cut-off values. This would eliminate any arbitrary and capricious assignment of values based on personal preference.*

I have run long already, but I must tell you that I enjoy your column and articles. I'm anxiously awaiting your forthcoming book.

Sincerely,
Joe LaGuerra
Roslyn Hts., NY

Answer: I have printed your entire letter because so much thought has obviously gone into it and some very good points have been brought out. I would like to say, however, that from my point of view, you are "spinning your wheels" somewhat in spending so much time on a standard, for it is my belief a standard is superfluous when you are breeding for a shadowy trait like gameness. It takes all your attention just to get and keep that elusive quality. Although there is variation in the breed, the Pit Bull is reasonably stable physically, as it has remained within the same rather broad physical parameters for hundreds of years. Now having said that, I'll try to make at least half-way sensible comments on your questions!

**Wilder's
Pankin**

(1) One of many problems that we get with standards is that it is hard to "nail down" exact meanings. For example, who knows what "bricklike" is intended to mean? Even so, I think "wedgelike" would be the more appropriate term, although a variety of shapes could fall under this category.
(2) In my opinion, a stop is of little consequence.
(3) I would tend to go with the old standard here.
(4) I would say medium. A short-necked dog is usually at a disadvantage.
(5) While most Pit Bull enthusiasts are tolerant about whether or not a dog has an ear trim, most of them will not even consider the docking of tails, I suppose just on the basis of tradition.

(6) Obviously, whoever made out the new standard was not overly familiar with the strains of Pit Bulls. It would be downright ludicrous to have one of the most prestigious strains in all Pit Bull history be discriminated against!

(7) I would very definitely be against holding the A.P.B.T. to that height range.

(8) It is an interesting point, but I am not aware of a limiting optimal weight in the Pit Bull. Maybe that's because the breed has a tendency to run small. The 80-pound dogs are impressive, but they are in the minority.

Question: *I love the A.P.B.T., Bull Terriers, Staffs, etc., and I wouldn't own any other breed. I would like to know if there is any way or do you know anyone who knows how to train the A.P.B.T. to get along with other dogs. If not the males (which I would prefer), is it possible with a bitch?*

Fred Nemiroff
Brooklyn, NY

Answer: Your best bet would be with a bitch, and even here you might be in trouble. I suppose a dog could be negatively conditioned to fighting by the use of an electric "stinger," but that strikes me as being akin to kicking a bird dog on point! A vet once told me that he successfully conditioned a Staff to not want to fight, but he ended up with a very unhappy and neurotic dog. The best solution is to keep your dog confined and on a leash.

Question: *I recently have been hearing a lot about the Chinese Fighting Dogs. I've read that there are over 50 presently in this country. How does this dog stand up or compare to the A.P.B.T.?*

Claudio DeGiffarde
New York, NY

Answer: The Chinese Fighting Dog has been in the country off and on for at least 20 years. It is interesting to note the different path that was taken in its development. The

Kelly's Gizmo

American (Pit) Bull Terrier was developed by simply breeding dogs on the basis of their performance and success. The Chinese Fighting Dog was apparently developed "blue print" style by putting together a breed with the traits you mentioned because, it was assured, they would be invaluable features for a fighting dog. In this case, apparently, the simple approach was the best, for the Chinese Fighting Dog has been a laughingstock against the Pit Bull.

Chapter Nine

OF BREAKING STICKS, PEDI-IGREES, AND TREADMILLS

Few men own their own property. The property owns them.
                                        —Robert G. Ingersol

Recently, a lot of grumbling was evoked from Pit Bull fanciers when *Bloodlines Journal* refused to carry advertisements for breaking sticks or treadmills. While the vast majority of Pit Bull people (probably over 90 percent) never contest their dogs in any kind of pit match, their attitude toward the activity varies. Some are very strongly opposed to the contests, but it is my impression that most are to some degree sympathetic with the activity, mainly because, knowing the dogs as they do, they can't see the cruelty allegations. And they are all-too-aware that the breed's gameness would be lost if not tested in the pit. In any case, most fanciers felt betrayed by *Bloodlines* when that magazine stopped accepting the advertisements. It was argued that a treadmill was only a means of exercising a dog, and the device is used by many non-pit dog people. And it was further stated, a breaking stick is to *stop* a fight, and every Staff and Bull Terrier person should have a set of these, too. Well...I agree. But now is a good time to give a little background on the United Kennel Club and its relationship to the American Pit Bull Terrier, and this may help put the whole problem into perspective.

The United Kennel Club was founded in 1898 by Chauncy Z. Bennett, and the first breed to be recognized was the American Pit Bull Terrier. Now Mr. Bennett was not a pit dog man in the sense that he ever matched dogs, but he was an enthusiastic promoter of the breed. He was not fool enough to fall for that absurd idea sometimes promulgated by kennel clubs that a breed is not a pure breed unless it is registered. He knew that the breeders of the Pit Bull often kept meticulous records, and not only did they keep the breed pure, they rarely bred outside their own strain. However, for sale to the general public, registration and a formal pedigree had come to be expected, and Mr. Bennett felt that the breed needed that in order to become popular. He also believed, and I think rightly so, that the dogs would benefit from U.K.C. sanctioned pit rules and from having matches presided over by a U.K.C.-licensed referee. Thus came into being the United Kennel Club Pit Rules that are still occasionally used by pit dog men today—much to the embarrassment of the U.K.C.! The rules are:

RULES GOVERNING RECOGNIZED PIT CONTESTS

WHEREAS. It is the aim of the United Kennel Club Registering Office, its members and the Pit Bull Terrier Fraternity, to place "Pit Contest" upon a recognized plane of excellence and promote more and better contests, the following rules have been adopted by the Fraternity and the United Kennel Club Registering Offices.

ONE. Pit contest to be recognized must employ a U. K. C. licensed Referee.

TWO. The principals may select any licensed U. K. C. Referee in good standing.

THREE. The Principals may select any fancier for the official timekeeper, but such selection must meet with the approval of the Referee.

FOUR. A licensed referee shall not preside over any "Pit Contest" where one or both of the combat dogs are non-U.K.C. registered "Cur" bloodlines.

FIVE. The combat dogs must be U. K. C. registered in their rightful owner's names and the Referee shall make sure of this and be in possession of their Registration Certificates during the contest.

SIX. The Referee shall deliver to the United Kennel

Hammond's
Bruno

Club Registering Offices a full and complete report of the contest within five (5) days after the contest.

SEVEN. Any Dog winning three (3) moneyed contests held under these rules and presided over by a U. K. C. licensed Referee, shall have the degree of Champion conferred upon him by the United Kennel Club Registering Offices and the Pit Bull Terrier Fraternity.

EIGHT. It shall be the duty of the official timekeeper to keep a correct record of the time consumed in the contest by scratch, and the number of scratches, etc., and he shall deliver the original time sheet (or a duplicate) to the Referee immediately after the contest to be sent to the United Kennel Club Registering Offices for record. It shall also be the duty of the official time keeper to call to the Referee before the scratch twenty-five (25) seconds "Get Ready", and thirty (30) seconds "Let Go", and the Referee shall act accordingly.

Hammond's Bull Plug carries his favorite toy—a bull's skull!

NINE. The full amount of the contest money shall be in the hands of the final stake holder before the Referee orders the dogs weighed. The Referee shall order the dogs weighed one (1) hour before the contest and they shall be weighed in the presence of the Referee and the final stake holder and either Dog exceeding the weight specified in the agreement shall forfeit then and there to his opponent all money posted.

TEN. After weighing the Dogs the Referee shall toss a coin for the Principals and the Principal winning the toss shall have his choice of having his dog washed (first or last) also his choice of corner in the "Pit."

ELEVEN. Each Principal shall furnish a sponge and two towels for washing and drying his Opponent's Dog. Both Dogs shall be washed in the center of the "Pit" with warm water and washing soda. Fifteen (15) minutes shall be allowed each Principal to wash his opponent's Dog. The time between washing each dog shall not exceed five (5) minutes and the washing of both dogs thirty-five (35) minutes.

TWELVE. After washing and drying, each Dog shall be placed in the hands of a watchful fancier in the corner of the "Pit" selected or assigned to him and kept there until the Principals are given the word "Let Go" by the Referee. Each Principal shall "let go" his opponent's Dog at the start and thereafter shall handle his own dog.

THIRTEEN. There shall be only one container of water in the "Pit" for sponging between a "pick up" and a "scratch" and each Principal shall furnish a sponge and two towels for sponging and drying his dog. The Referee shall examine the sponges and water and have full charge of them at all times.

FOURTEEN. It shall be a fair "scratch in turn" contest. Thirty (30) seconds shall be allowed between every "pick up" and "scratch", twenty-five (25) seconds for sponging, drying and fanning, and five (5) seconds to get ready.

FIFTEEN. To establish a fair "turn" which will entitle either Principal to "pick up". Both dogs must be free from holds and the dog which is accused of "turning" must have turned his head and shoulders from his opponent. Either Principal upon noticing this action may appeal to the Referee and claim the "Turn" and if the claim be just and fair the referee shall immediately call a "pick up" and notify the other Principal it is his turn to scratch.

SIXTEEN. At twenty-five (25) seconds the Referee shall call "get ready" and at thirty (30) seconds he shall call "let go" and the Principal of the Dog to scratch shall take his hands off his dog fair inside of his "scratch line" and to be a fair "scratch" his dog must go across the "Pit" inside his opponent's "scratch line" and mouth his opponent. Should the Dog fail to go across and mouth his opponent he loses the contest and the Referee shall immediately announce the winner.

SEVENTEEN. While one Dog is "scratching" the opponent shall hold his dog's head and shoulders fair between his legs just inside his "scratch line".

EIGHTEEN. Should a Dog while "scratching" become

confused and sway to either side of a direct line to his opponent as long as he does not turn his head away from his opponent he is making a fair "scratch".

NINETEEN. Should any outsider attract the Dog's attention while "scratching" and the Dog, stop, or "scratch" the article or object instead of his opponent, the Referee shall immediately order the Dog "Scratched" over.

TWENTY. Should either dog become fanged, the referee shall order a "pick up" and allow the principal to unfang his dog, then immediately order them put down two feet apart and give the word "let go". This action does not have any connection with a "Turn" or "Scratch" and must not be considered so. Principals can un-fang their Dogs with their hands without picking them up if the Referee so decides.

Hammond's Booker T, inbred grandson of the Plumbers' "Alligator"

TWENTY-ONE. Should a fair "Turn and Pick Up" be made and the Dogs accidentally get in hold again, the Refferee shall order them parted and proceed in thirty (30) seconds with the "scratch".

TWENTY-TWO. Principals shall be allowed to encourage their Dogs by voice and actions. Should a Principal touch either dog with his hand, foot or other article while in action the referee shall immediately call a foul and announce his opponent the winner.

TWENTY-THREE. Principals shall take their hands off their Dog fair inside their "scratch line". Should a Principal push his Dog over his "scratch line" the referee shall immediately call a foul and announce his opponent the winner.

TWENTY-FOUR. Should a Principal pick his Dog up without being told to by the referee, the Referee shall immediately call a foul and announce his opponent the winner.

TWENTY-FIVE. Should a Principal leave his corner before the Dogs have resumed action, the referee shall immediately call a foul and announce his opponent the winner.

TWENTY-SIX. Under no circumstances where a match is made and money posted, shall the money be returned without a contest. The Principal appearing for the contest shall be declared the winner and receive the "stake" money.

TWENTY-SEVEN. Should interference of any kind prevent a fair decisive contest, the Principals and the Referee shall name the next time and place for the contest (within fifteen (15) days.) Should the Principals and the Referee fail to agree upon the future meeting place, it shall then be the duty of the Referee to name the time and place and the same referee shall preside over this unfinished contest and the Principals and Referee shall start this contest with "Rule 3".

TWENTY-EIGHT. Any persons or persons found guilty of doping, faking, poisoning or attempting to dope, fake, poison or damage any dog or dogs, before, during or after the contest, shall forfeit all money, fined $100 and be barred from the Pit Bull Terrier fraternity for a period of three (3) years, and a full report of such action shall be printed two times each year for a period of three (3) years in the June and December issues of the United Kennel Club official Journal, Bloodlines.

TWENTY-NINE. In all recognized contests the decisions of the U.K.C. licensed Referee shall be final and all bets shall go as the "main stakes".

THIRTY. The "Pit" shall be 16 ft. square with sides two and one half feet high, with a tight wood floor. A line shall be painted across the center, also a scratch line painted across each Principal's corner. To draw this scratch line, measure 7 feet out each way from the corner.

THIRTY-ONE. These rules may be amended or altered by a two-thirds vote of the Fraternity at any meeting of the Fraternity, providing notice of such amendments or alterations and their nature has been given the Fraternity at least thirty (30) days previous to such meeting and such alterations and amendments must meet with the approval of the Fraternity which are Members of the United Kennel Club Registering offices, before they shall be adopted.

Blair's Jude, from heavy "Dibo" breeding

DIMENSIONS OF THE DOG PIT

CIRCULAR PIT—Twenty-four feet round, eight feet in diameter, thirty inches high, when the boards are straight.

SQUARE PIT— 16 feet square, thirty-six inches high, with a border of three and one-half inches wide, of Virginia pine; the boards grooved.

Fourteen feet square with sides two feet high.

Wallace's Red Rustler

The United Kennel Club struggled at first, and the Pit Bull fanciers were not much help really. Many of the breeders still did not register their dogs because it went against a basic tradition to keep secret pedigrees. Part of the game was to know all about the other guy's breeding without having him know anything about yours! And, too, many breeders were not happy with the name, as they had been used to calling the dogs simply "Bulldogs." When the United Kennel Club really hit paydirt was when they began registering coonhounds. The coonhound people had not wanted their dogs registered with the American Kennel Club because they identified that outfit strictly with show dogs, yet they wanted the status of a registry, so they took to the U.K.C. like long-lost children. The U.K.C. was now completely solvent, and a magazine called *Bloodlines Journal* was established and went out to those who did business with the registry.

Throughout the United Kennel Club's long history, the American Pit Bull Terrier breed has been more of a problem than anything else to the organization. However, despite numerous problems, Mr. Bennett stood steadfastly by the breed. After his death in 1936, the organization was taken over by his daughter, and later her husband gave up his medical practice to help her with the business. Under their direction, *Bloodlines* became more restrictive regarding the APBT. The breed was moved from the front of the magazine to the back. Advertisements announcing that dogs were open to match were no longer accepted, and the magazine would no longer carry accounts of matches. These changes took place over a long period of time, and they were in response to pressures utilized by the other large registry which could always discredit the United Kennel Club simply by characterizing it as an advocate of dogfighting.

Reaction from Pit Bull fanciers was as bitter as it was predictable. Most fanciers seemed to feel that the American Pit Bull Terrier breed had "carried" the U.K.C. through hard times, and now that the organization had coonhounds and other breeds, it was betraying its original benefactor. The truth is, as already mentioned, the U.K.C. never got full benefit of the Pit Bull transactions because many breeders kept private pedigrees, and others registered their dogs with the American Dog Breeders Association, which registered Pit Bulls only and was an unswerving advocate of pit fights. However, there were some legitimate complaints. For one thing, the American Kennel Club had opened its stud books to the breed for a year or so, but most APBT fanciers did not take advantage of the opportunity strictly out of loyalty to the U.K.C. Also, some fanciers pointed out that the coonhunts and field trials that were dutifully reported in every issue of *Bloodlines* were better candidates for a charge of cruelty to animals than were pit contests. They argued that it was common practice for the dogs to kill a coon, and in such a situation, you had an intelligent animal that was fighting out of absolute terror. In a pit contest, they argued, there was no cruelty, for the dogs had been bred for centuries to like what they did. If a dog wanted to quit, the battle was over right there and then. It was also pointed out that an interest in pit dogs was no more indicative of a vicious nature than an interest in racing pigeons of an aeronautical inclination. Well, anyway, the debate was interesting. But the United Kennel Club completed its transformation, and for well over twenty years now it has disassociated itself from pit contests completely. It now provides a forum in *Bloodlines* only for those fanciers who are interested in the breed as a guard, a pet, a catch dog or a hunter.

In spite of its present policy, many ignoramuses continue to project the image of the United Kennel Club as a pit organization. The sad fact is that the U.K.C. has had to suf-

Garcia's Chato, son of Wallace's Bad Red

fer the harassment of having all the Pit Bull people mad at it for not supporting the contests or even allowing paid advertising to enable reputable breeders to answer ridiculous stories that were carried in the news media, and at the same time face the ire of all those who mistakenly believe that the U.K.C. is in support of pit contests. Fred Miller, the current president of the U.K.C., once told me that the vaguest report of a pit contest that appears in print is occasion for him to receive several clippings of the report from all over the country, along with indignant letters wanting to know what he is doing about such goings on.

Komosinski's Cap, owned by Jeff Kuhns

And that brings us back to the reason that *Bloodlines* has refused advertising space for breaking sticks and treadmills. The organization is under such pressure that it has to avoid even the appearance of any association whatsoever with pit fighting.

It is certainly true, however, that breaking sticks are the humane way to stop a dog fight. Most people automatically start to beat on the dogs to break them up. Others turn the hose on them, build fires under their noses, and even throw scalding water on them. None of these methods works with the Pit Bull. I am often astonished at the injuries people will subject dogs to merely to break up a fight. I recently read a book by a well-known authority on hunting dogs, and in the book he told of two occasions in which a couple of his dogs got into fights. On one occasion our "expert" separated the dogs by kicking one dog in the ribs while throttling the other with a choke chain! On the other, he brained one of the dogs with a heavy object. What this dog authority needed to know was that dogs are not capable of damaging each other as much as most people think. Stories of slit throats and disembowelments are just that, stories told by imaginative authors. So there is no need to panic the way everybody does. Only if there is great disparity in size is there any immediate danger to one of the combatants. Knowing this, we can proceed in a more calm and logical manner to separate a pair of fighting dogs. What is needed is a breaking stick. This is simply a stick made of soft wood and shaped like a knife. Two

Trussell's Dum Dum, 85 pounds, heavy "Dibo" breeding

people are needed to part the dogs. Each person takes his dog by the scruff of the neck (not the collar, for that will choke the dog). The dogs, being Pit Bulls, will not want you to separate them, and will hold on to each other. Insert the breaking stick behind the eye teeth and begin working it into the mouth with a rockingchair prying motion. One of the dogs will probably come loose before the other, and it is important to keep that breaking stick in his mouth to keep him from grabbing the other dog again. With Pit Bulls, you don't have to worry about one of them

Reed's Babu Dibeau, 58 pounds

147

biting you—at least not on purpose! But if your dog has hold of some other breed, make sure the other guy keeps that breaking stick in the other dog's mouth, or he is likely to bite *both* of you! If it is a fight between two dogs of breeds other than Pit Bulls, or possibly Staffs or Bull Terriers, chances are they will soon quit on their own after they begin to tire.

The injuries a dog gets from a fight may look bad but will heal quickly and not amount to very much. Broken bones are rare—in fact, extremely rare—but even this injury is not a serious danger to a dog's life. The greatest danger is shock, especially if your dog has gotten hold of a dog that is not a Pit Bull, as dogs of other breeds go into shock easily. Pit Bulls resist shock very well, and they are excellent healers. And they don't seem to suffer much, if at all, during recuperation. However, even though he is hard to hurt and hard to kill, shock is the greatest danger to a Pit Bull, too. The following is an excellent article on shock that appeared in the pit dog magazine called the *Sporting Dog Journal.*

Hammond's Tuffy, pure Heinzl breeding

FLUID THERAPY FOR TREATING
HYPO-VOLEMIC SHOCK *
By: Jack Kelly

Although the by-line on this article is credited to Jack
Kelly, let me make it clear that I am only assembling this
article from detailed conversations with several veterinarians who would, for obvious reasons, prefer that their
names not be used in this publication.

The word "hypo-volemic" when broken down becomes
self-explanatory. *Hypo* meaning under, *volemic,* as in vol-
ume. It means that the shock is caused by a severe loss of
body fluid. Therefore the remedy is obvious: replace those
lost body fluids as quickly as possible to prevent the shock
from becoming irreversible.

Anyone who is actively matching dogs has a basic
knowledge of how to treat the visible signs that are the results of a hard-fought contest. Lacerations, puncture
wounds and the like are easy enough to treat, and then it
just becomes a matter of keeping the wounds freè of infec-
tion, and it's seldom that a dog dies as a result of that type
of injury. Shock is something else and is usually the reason why the dog dies.

Of course, the best thing you can do for a dog in shock is
to get him to a qualified veterinarian, but as we all know,
most times that's not possible. The next best thing to do is
exactly what a veterinarian would do for the dog if you
had been able to get him to one, and this article will attempt to explain that procedure.

Let us say that your dog has just won a long, hard-
fought battle. He is exhausted and could barely stand to
make his last scratch. You take him from the pit and he's
cool and clammy to the touch, his breathing is shallow and
his eyes are glazed over. He is in hypo-volemic shock, and
if something isn't done to replace the body fluids he has
lost in that long, hard fight, the shock will advance to a
point where it becomes irreversible and the dog will surely
die.

The best way to get the fluid back into the dog is by in-

* Appeared in the January-February, 1974 issue of *Sporting Dog Journal.*

travenous feeding. To do this you will need some special equipment, none of which is expensive. (1) a venoclysis set, which is merely the tubing and valve, that is commonly referred to as an IV set. (2) a 20 to 23 gauge needle and detachable syringe. (3) two 500cc bottles of lactated ringers, which is the fluid that you will feed intravenously to the dog and (4) a roll of adhesive tape. All of this equipment can be purchased at any medical or veterinarian supply company. If you do have difficulty buying this equipment, the *Sporting Dog Journal* can get it for you.

The most difficult part of setting up an intravenous feeding into a dog in shock is to find a suitable vein and setting the needle into that vein. The large vein running the length of either front leg is the best one to try first. Many times the vein will have collapsed, and it will take some doing to get the vein set up for feeding. After the dog has been taken from the pit, wrapped in a blanket and made as comfortable as possible, then hang the 500cc bottle of lactated ringers higher than where the dog is lying, open the venoclysis set and place the larger end into the rubber end of the lactated ringers bottle; make sure the valve on

Sorrell's Ra Ja

Hammond's Willie

the venoclysis set is in the "off" position. Now to find the vein—have an assistant or someone willing to help grasp the dog's leg ABOVE the elbow and squeeze, in effect applying a tourniquet with his hand while at the same time forcing the leg to straighten at the elbow; the leg must be straight and not bent at the elbow. As the vein swells, it is held between the finger tips, which circle the dog's leg from underneath. If the vein is so depleted that it doesn't show up under the skin, squeeze the foot several times and try to pump the blood into that section of the vein that you intend to use. When the vein swells and becomes visible under the skin, thread the needle under the skin and up into the vein and pull back on the plunger of the syringe; if you are in the vein, you will draw a small amount of blood into the syringe. Once you are satisfied that the needle is correctly set, tape it to the leg with the adhesive tape. Your assistant can now release his tourniquet from the dog's leg, disconnect the syringe from the needle and connect the venoclysis tube to the needle. Tape the tubing also to the leg and open the valve on the venoclysis to the fully OPEN position. Allow the entire 500cc bottle to empty into the dog and then connect the second bottle of lactated ringers to the venoclysis set and give him a total of 1000cc.

In some cases, you will not be able to raise the vein and will be unable to set up the IV feeding. As a last resort you can take a 50cc syringe and inject it just under the skin of the dog, preferably in the area of the abdomen, and push as much of the fluid into him as you can, making sure to massage the swelling on the surface of the dog's skin that results from the fluid's being injected in that manner.

The veterinarians that I spoke to estimate that injecting the fluid under the skin is only 20% as effective as intravenous feeding, so make every effort to raise the vein. If you have trouble raising the vein, try the other side and in the meantime start the injections under the skin, but don't give up trying to get the venoclysis set in operation.

If at all possible, talk this procedure over with an understanding veterinarian. Learn the technique of raising that big vein in the front leg, and remember the leg has to be straight until the needle is in place and taped to the leg. If the leg is bent at the elbow, the vein will "float" in the leg and be just that much harder to thread a needle into.

If the shock becomes irreversible or is irreversible before you take the dog from the pit, then of course the dog must die, but there is no way to tell at what point the shock is irreversible, so get the fluid into him as soon as possible. If the dog can and will lap up water, let him have it; put a small amount of salt in the water. Once the dog's kidneys are functioning, then you have just about got it made.

With a little effort on your part, the dog can be given the same care that he would receive at the hands of a qualified veterinarian. The procedure isn't simple and does take some practice, but if it saves the life of one game dog, it is well worth the time you spend learning how to do it.

In conjunction with fluid therapy, there is one other

thing that can help save a dog, the use of a trachea tube, or a breathing tube inserted into the dog's trachea, with which you can help him get air into his lungs.

TREADMILLS

Treadmills are especially handy to have for Pit Bulldogs, because typical individuals of the breed love exercise but can't be allowed to run at large. Almost all Bulldogs are bears for work and love to run a treadmill. I would once again like to draw on *Sporting Dog Journal* for a very fine article on treadmills.

USE OF THE TREADMILL* by Jack Kelly

The treadmill is probably the most maligned and at the same time the most over-rated piece of training equipment used in exercising pit dogs. Just about every conditioning method published over the past 75 years has included in it some treadmill work. The Armitage book, the Colby book, Jack Manweiler's article on conditioning, written around the turn of the century and printed in *Bloodlines Journal* in 1940, and Ed Palmer's article on conditioning published in *Pit Dog Magazine* (Sept. 1959) and reprinted in *Sporting Dog Journal* (Nov.-Dec. 1973) all recommended treadmill work of from 20 minutes to one hour for maximum results in building stamina. In discussing treadmill work with other dog men, some claim a short wind sprint of 12 to 14 minutes is best, while others claim prolonged runs up to 2 hours and 45 minutes will get the best results. Obviously, both cannot be correct for your dog, so what is the correct amount of time to work a dog up to during conditioning? There are many factors that you should consider to determine the right amount of work for your particular dog, and this article will discuss them.

First of all, let me point out that many first class dog conditioners do not even use a treadmill, so it is not an absolute necessity to use one; however, in urban areas, where roading a dog next to a car or bicycle is impractical or there are just not enough long grassy meadows for walking, a treadmill is just about indispensable.

We all know what a treadmill is, so it won't be neces-

* Appeared in the January-February, 1975 issue of *Sporting Dog Journal.*

Putting two mills in position so that the dogs are facing each other makes the "millwork" even more enjoyable for the dogs.

sary to go into the construction of one, other than to say it is a continuous belt on which a dog can run at his own pace. One of the first things you should take into consideration is how easy or hard your mill is to turn. Naturally, a dog working on a hard-turning mill can't work as long as he could on a real easy-turning mill. In the Armitage book, the author advises mill work up to 45 minutes and in another section of the book he has a picture of the treadmill he owned and used, a wood slat belt running over rollers and apparently easy to turn. In the Colby book, the author limits the amount of mill work to 20 minutes, but Colby made a mill on which a carpet slid over a graphite treated wood slide, and it was a much harder mill for a dog to work on. So while the amount of time differs greatly, the ease with which the mill operates has a great deal to do with the time difference. Therefore you should determine how hard your mill is to work; if it rolls easily to the touch, your dog could conceivably work it for a longer period of time without exhausting himself than on a mill that is stiff and requires more effort to turn.

Next let's take into consideration the dog that is going to work on your particular mill. They come in all shapes and sizes; some are lazy, some are eager, some aren't going to work a mill no matter what you do, others will jump up on one and start to work before you can get a harness on him. It's nothing more than common sense, then, to realize that a dog that runs a mill flat out won't have to stay on one to get as much out of it as a dog that just walks along on it. A dog that simply walks a mill might well be able to stay at it for 2 hours and 45 minutes, while the eager worker could run himself to death in less than an hour. Of course, those are the two extremes; most of our dogs fit in somewhere in between. The point I'm trying to make is that the speed at which your dog works the mill should play a large part in your determining what is the correct time to work him on your treadmill.

Carpet-type mill on the left and a "slat" mill on the right

Another thing to consider is how your dog has been exercised prior to getting him into condition for a match. The dog that has been brought up on a treadmill from the time he's a pup is naturally going to be able to tolerate a lot more mill work during conditioning than the dog that never saw a mill until you have started conditioning him. Many men have made the mistake of taking a dog that has never been on a treadmill and then expecting him in 6 or 7 weeks to get into condition relying primarily on the treadmill. If you have a dog that won't work a mill or has never been on a mill, or if you don't know what his early training has been, you are better off relying on something else, such as roadwork, rather than prolonged running on a mill.

So with those basic facts in mind you begin to work your dog for a match and you are planning on using a treadmill. You have your dog thinned out some and not obese, because you should never run a fat dog on a mill. So with a combination of proper diet and lots of hand walking you determine that he's ready for the treadmill. After taking your dog for a good long walk to get him empty, you put a hardness on him and let him run the mill for about three minutes. The dog will probably wind sprint those three minutes, but don't let that encourage you to work him any harder. Take him off the mill, walk him until he's cooled off, rub him down and put him in his quarters. Each succeeding day, you let him run a little longer. If he's working particuarly well one day, let him increase his mill time by about five minutes; if he's not working well, take him off. Millwork has to be a gradual thing, increasing each day's work a few minutes at a time. If for any reason he doesn't look as if he's enjoying his work, rest him; don't be in a hurry to force him to work on the mill. After several days on the mill, he will be up to about twenty minutes at a time, and you should be taking special care to watch for any signs of undue fatigue. If his breathing is abnormally labored or his running is forced, you are better off taking him off the mill rather than risking overworking him. It's always a good idea to watch the dog's hind legs as he runs.

He should be picking them up and moving freely. Once he starts to drag his back legs, he's definitely had too much. Before long you will know when your dog has had enough work for that particular day.

Used properly, a treadmill is an invaluable piece of training equipment, but it's also the easiest way in the world to overwork a dog.

THE SPRINGPOLE

Another item that is often used is called a springpole. (Incidentally, I should mention here that while all of the paraphernalia was originally designed to condition a dog for the pit, it is all also used by people who keep the dogs strictly as pets. It is fun to watch the enthusiasm of the dogs at work, and it keeps them in shape.) The arrangement is a long sapling pole propped up from the ground near its base. A rope hangs from the end of the pole with a

"Cobra" testing a springpole-like device put out by the Pit Stop Leather Company.

Wallace's Fancy and Wallace's Dude as pups

hide dangling from it. A Pit Bull loves to jump up and grab the hide, hang from it, and shake it (or shake himself, since he is hanging from the hide!). A more common setup is to suspend a rope from a tree, tie it to a garage door-type spring, then run some more rope down to the hide. As far as that goes, it is not even necessary to have a hide or coonskin, as a pair of old overalls will do almost as well!

Earlier on in this book reference was made to the use of a chain as opposed to kennel runs for keeping a Pit Bull. Kennel runs are an expensive proposition, and I've always disliked the way a dog has a tendency to run through his own fecal matter. The wider-type runs help prevent this, but then these are even more expensive. Pit Bulls have been kept on chains for so long (hundreds of years probably) that they seem philosophical about being so kept. A major hazard in keeping a dog in this way is that the dog may end up hanging himself if you are not careful. You must be sure not to put him near a fence or any other obstacle that he may jump over and thus hang himself. The ideal setup, in my opinion, is the cable system that has

Sequan Invictus, son of Going Light Barney,
half-grown

Longello's Skipper, leaping
for a "hide"

Sorrell's Red Jerry

Sequan Mike

King's Semo

Sequan Willie and Jones's Tuffy as puppies

Irish Pagan

been employed by some fanciers. A cable is strung from tree to tree (or posts), and a pulley is put on the cable and a heavy chain is run down from that.

Of course, a large yard is perfectly adequate for just one dog as long as it is fenced in. If you have an excitable male dog, however, he will very likely find a way to climb or jump the fence when he sees another dog. So you may want to have a kennel run or chain for him while you are gone, just for your own peace of mind. To be fair to the breed, I should mention that most people I know that have raised these dogs as house pets and guards have not had this kind of problem. The dog raised in this way seems to be less likely, for some reason, to try to break out, even when excited by another dog's presence outside. Still, the keeping of a Pit Bull is a serious responsibility that requires the owner to have an appreciation of the breed. I once attempted to express the reasons that form the basis for my own attraction to the breed. I would like to end this book with that article.

Wise's Max Jr.

**Wise's Tiger
Babe,
50 pounds,
daughter of
Wise's Max**

Wallace's Bad Red

WHAT ARE THEY GOOD FOR? *

Although the American (Pit) Bull Terrier's very existence is being intensely questioned today in some quarters, such controversy is nothing new for the breed. Ancient writings (in Middle English, no less) contain passages that decry the fact that the Bulldog was allowed to exist because, it was maintained, the breed was merely an engine of destruction. Well, my friends (both ancient and modern!), I can sympathize with you and understand why you feel the way you do, but you simply do not know the breed! It would be hard to find a dog with a more dependable disposition with people. If raised in the house from puppyhood, a Pit Bull will be a delightful house pet, amusing, roguish, and unbelievably lovable. Okay, so they're fine pets, but what else are they good for? (Somehow, people demand more of the APBT!) Well, let's see now. . . .

Of course, they are "naturals" as guard dogs, in which their gameness and forbidding appearance come into play.

* Appeared in the July-August, 1975 issue of *Bloodlines Journal.*

Dibeaus Boozer at 3½ months

Some of us who know of the APBT's great love for people may question whether most members of the breed would attack a human. Would an APBT possibly be one of those proverbial dogs that lick the burglar's hand and point the way to the silverware and other valuables? Apparently not, for as one writer said, the APBT is the canine Will Rogers. He is a friend to everybody until or unless a person proves he is *not* a friend. I have heard stories over and over of how a Pit Bull that had been everybody's friend somehow knew when it was time to stop being so friendly. My own boyhood Pit Bull rose to the occasion when our house was broken into. Before that time (and after) he never bothered a soul!

The only American (Pit) Bull Terrier that I ever knew that was actually trained to do guard work was a pup I sold named "Willie," and he proved to be a smashing success in the highly-respected and rigorous *Schutzhund* guard dog program. He is owned by Bill and Gail Ross of Sequan Kennels.

The American (Pit) Bull Terrier is also well known as a catch dog, and this is another activity in which the breed absolutely reigns supreme. In fact, I don't know of a single other breed that has been used consistently or successfully. For "city slickers" who don't know what a catch dog is, let me explain. Usually, catch dogs are utilized on open ranges in which hogs or cattle are allowed to run free. The problem for the rancher is that when it comes time to catch a particular animal, it usually turns out to be a rather difficult feat, especially in rough terrain with heavy brush. Difficult, that is, unless you have a catch dog. In that case, you simply indicate the animal to your APBT, and he "catches" him. The dogs get very clever at what they do, but it remains a job that very definitely belongs in the "tough" category, for the dogs are dealing with animals many times their size. If the animal is a boar, the dog usually catches him by the ear. If it is a steer, the nose is the preferred hold. Once the animal is tired or subdued, the owner can slip a rope on a leg and call off the dog. (Yes, the catch dogs I've seen actually could be called off with a mere "That'll do." Obviously, careful selection and a lot of training were involved.)

The American (Pit) Bull Terrier is also good as a hunting dog, specifically as a "still trailer" (a dog that does not bay on the trail). To appreciate the significance of this, let's first consider the function of the so-called "open trailer" (the dog that bays while trailing). Both types are ably described in Dr. Leon Whitney's fine book on coonhunting (*The Coonhunters Handbook*). Complaining that most hound men have an inflated idea of a wild animal's tricks to elude the hounds, Whitney describes a raccoon's typical meanderings, up and down trees, and making a zig-zag path before he even hears the dogs.

Sequan Willie (son of Wallace's Bad Red) was the outstanding attack dog of his *Schutzhund* class.

According to Dr. Whitney, the extra utility of the still trailer to the hunter is that the raccoon does not get much advance warning that something is out to get him. Instead of hearing a lot of barking and yapping off in the distance, he is suddenly confronted with a raging canine that has approached him on the sneak; he has to beat a very quick retreat and therefore has to be a lot less choosy about picking his refuge. He can't amble over to the nearest big tree and climb up, because he doesn't have time for any ambling, being in a desperate full flight. Therefore the hunter is benefited, because the raccoon is forced into a much less secure refuge, making his capture easier. Dr. Whitney also points out that most coon hunters have the wrong idea about the effect of the open trailer's baying. It doesn't panic the raccoon at all; he's heard it all before and is not about to be panicked and steered away from his normal

Rowell's Baby Doll, 45 pounds, a very fine "catch dog"

Riptide Belle

leisurely routine just because some hot-headed hound is doing a lot of screaming in the background. So he just keeps going along at his regular pace, keeping an ear cocked to make sure that the dogs don't get too close. When they get close enough for him to be concerned, he picks himself out a nice tall tree and lodges in it.

Dr. Whitney has, in other books, recommended the APBT as the best of the still trailers. To be perfectly honest, though, it may take the infusion of some hound blood to make sure the dog has a good nose. Many Pit Bulls do not have the desire to trail, but it is certainly true that many of them do.

In addition to serving as (1) a fine house pet, (2) a personal, business, or house guard, (3) a catch dog, and (4) a hunting dog, the breed serves as a reservoir of pure courage into which breeders may (and have many times) dip into to "stiffen" the backbones of their own breeds. For that very reason, our breed has been involved in the manufacture of many new breeds. To name just a few in which our breed has been accredited a major role (although, as always, there is controversy as to the actual origin of these breeds), there is the plucky little Boston Terrier (whose originators wanted to call it the Boston *Bull* Terrier!), the Plott Hound, the renowned Mountain Cur, The Bull Terrier, the Staffordshire Bull Terrier, and so forth.

Even if the Pit Bull served no purpose, he would be worth preserving as a relic of the ages that has come down to us virtually unchanged, with his great courage and magnificent gameness still intact. But, happily, he does have his practical uses. In fact, there are more uses for the breed than I have taken time to tell about. And when your wife or daughter takes your APBT for a walk, you may rest assured that she is in safe hands!

ILLUSTRATIONS INDEX

INDEX

RED NOSE: A copper-colored nose usually shown by members of the Old Family Red Nose strain. (This nose coloration is also shown occasionally by dogs of other strains.)

ROLL: A practice or training bout.

SCRATCH: A method by which a dog must demonstrate his gameness in a pit contest. The scratch consists of a dog's crossing the pit and taking hold of his opponent within a specified count, which varies somewhat depending upon the rules of the match.

SCRATCH LINE: A line drawn diagonally across the corner of the pit over which the dog to scratch must not be placed before being released.

STAFFORDSHIRE BULL TERRIER: The English show version of the Pit Bull. It has been developed along different lines from the American Staffordshire Terrier, being smaller and having a squat appearance.

SPRING POLE: A device for exercising a Pit Bull. It involves a hide attached to a heavy spring or a sapling pole that the dog can jump up and grab.

TOSA: A large (up to 140 pounds) breed of Japanese fighting dog. It looks like a cross between a Pit Bull and a Mastiff.

TREADMILL: A device for running a dog in place. The two main types are carpet mills and slat mills.

TURN: A pit term that refers to a dog's turning his head and shoulders away from his opponent. The various sets of rules differ somewhat in describing a turn. Some define any turn away from the opponent as an official turn even if it is simply a manuever. Others specify that the dogs must be free of holds for a turn to be designated as such.

TURN TABLE: A type of treadmill, not too common now, that consists of a flat round surface that turns under the dog as he runs.

TUSK: Any of the four "canine" teeth. This term is an example of some of the archaic terms that persist as part of the Pit Bull culture that has been handed down through the ages.

UNITED KENNEL CLUB: The second largest dog registry in the country. The organization is privately owned and specializes in Coonhounds. It sponsors the American Pit Bull Terrier but discourages pit contests.

it belonged in a zoo, but they pronounced it "the best of the worst" and gleefully predicted the end of the Pit Bull. As it turned out, the breed was mere "cannon fodder" for the Pit Bull.

CUR: Two meanings: 1. Any dog of any breed other than the Pit Bull, and 2. Any dog (including Pit Bulls) that are not deeply game.

CUR OUT: To demonstrate a lack of gameness, to quit.

DUDLEY NOSE: A flesh-colored nose. (Note that this is absolutely not the same thing as a red nose!)

FULL DROP EARS: Ears that hang down all the way (like those of Colby's Pinscher).

GAME TEST: To ascertain the depth of a dog's gameness by rolling him until he is so tired and thirsty he can hardly stand, then allowing him to prove his gameness by scratching to a fresh dog.

KEEP: Another pit term that refers to the "training camp" of a Pit Bull that has been matched. A "keep" usually consists of isolating a dog from all possible stimuli and keeping him quiet except during his exercise periods.

NATURAL EARS: Uncropped ears. About half the American Pit Bull Terriers have uncropped ears, and most owners are erratic about whether ears should be cropped.

OLD FAMILY: A family of pit dogs that was imported from Ireland in the latter half of the last century. Examples of strains that were founded upon the Old Family were the Colby, Feeley, Lightner and Corvino bloodlines.

OLD FAMILY REDS: A segment of the Old Family that, when kept pure of all other lines, were either red, white, or red and white in color.

OLD FAMILY RED NOSE: A segment of the Old Family Red strain that when kept pure showed a red (or copper-colored) nose.

PIED: White with tan patches (with perhaps some darker colors mixed in). (Riptide Belle would be an example of a pied-colored dog.)

PIT WEIGHT: The fighting weight of a pit dog. The dogs are brought down to their most efficient weight for pit contests.

RED: The term "red" is used to refer to nearly any shade of fawn except the very light ones.

GLOSSARY

AMERICAN DOG BREEDERS ASSOCIATION: A registry that has existed since 1889 and caters only to the American Pit Bull Terrier. Unlike the United Kennel Club, it has not denounced pit contests.

AMERICAN STAFFORDSHIRE TERRIER: The show counterpart of the American Pit Bull Terrier The breed was formerly known as the Staffordshire Terrier, but "American" was later added to emphasize that this breed had developed along lines different from those of the Staffordshire Bull Terrier.

BAN DOG: A term used at one time for Bulldogs and Mastiffs. It has since been used for a newly created breed that was founded by crossing a Pit Bull with an Italian Mastiff.

BAT EARS: Erect ears, rounded at the top.

BREAKING STICK: A wedge-shaped stick used to "break" the hold of a Pit Bull in a fight.

CATCHWEIGHT: A heavyweight, any dog over 52 pounds pit weight.

BUCKSKIN: A very light fawn coloration. (The term "fawn" is rarely used as a color designation by Pit Bull fanciers.)

BUTTERFLY NOSE: A type of "dudley nose" in which there are some spots of pigment on the nose.

CATCH DOG: A dog that is used for catching wild boar and rough cattle. Such dogs are especially useful in brushy uneven terrain in which it is impractical to attempt to rope the animals. To my knowledge, no dog other than a Pit Bull has ever been very successful in this occupation.

CHAIN WEIGHT: The normal weight of a dog in a kennel, on a chain or (for house pets) in the house.

CHINESE FIGHTING DOG: A strange-looking dog, weighing about 50 pounds. The breed was obviously put together with traits that were assumed to be useful in a fight. The dog has a tough hide, a dense "inpenetrable" coat, loose skin (to allow it to turn and seize any dog that has hold of it), and huge curved fangs. The editors of a humane society bulletin once said that the Chinese Fighting Dog looked like